To, Phyllis

Life is a gift :)!

AN IRISH History

Maeve Omstead Johnston

Mawe

FriesenPress

Suite 300 - 990 Fort St
Victoria, BC, Canada, V8V 3K2
www.friesenpress.com

Copyright © 2015 by Maeve Omstead Johnston
First Edition — 2015

ISBN
978-1-4602-6255-9 (Hardcover)
978-1-4602-6256-6 (Paperback)
978-1-4602-6257-3 (eBook)

1. Fiction, Historical

Distributed to the trade by The Ingram Book Company

Acknowledgements

This story was written in memory of my mother, Margaret Elizabeth Hogg (McGrotty), whose storytelling and love of reading gave birth to my appreciation of literature, history and the written word.

I dedicate this book to my husband, Bob Johnston, whose encouragement, love, and strength anchor my life, inspire me and keep my heart singing.

Special thanks to my daughter-in-law, Sue, for her encouragement and editing skills.

With appreciation to my fellow authors: my son, Tom, and my dear friend, June Fleckenstein Emmert, for your ideas, editing assistance and moral support.

Thanks to all of my family for keeping my mind active, my editing and writing skills honed, and warming my heart with your love and thoughtfulness.

The ongoing friendship and love of innumerable friends and mentors provide me with the enthusiasm and inspiration to continue writing.

Foreword

It was a daydreamer's persistence that made the discovery of the New World a possibility, then a reality. The immigrants who travelled to this continent imagined life could be better for them. First they had the dream. Then they made plans and followed them through. History is documented by books, diaries, journals, logs, and storytellers.

Every family seems to have at least one gifted soul who has the ability, the patience and the literary skills to trace their ancestors. Many trips have been made to the 'old country' seeking distant cousins and dates on tombstones. I have great respect for these diligent people. We now live in a generation influenced by technology and have innumerable means available to trace family backgrounds.

This story is a tale that has been waiting a long time to be written. It is the story of a family who immigrated to Canada, seeking a more promising life. It was lived by the people described in it. The original storytellers passed their family histories from generation to generation by word-of-mouth. In the telling, each story was either enhanced or downplayed simply by the relator's ability to remember details. That is precisely the manner in which this story has been written.

My family's history has come to me by word-of-mouth from my mother and my aunts. The discrepancies in the reflections told by these individuals have intrigued me throughout the years. The story takes place from 1900 to 1952. Many of the events unfurled exactly as described. Personalities have been preserved, but some names have been changed. The storyline evolved from bedtime tales, letters, love, and the author's imagination.

Prologue

Life's circumstances forced Sean McGrotty's family apart, as desperation led him to leave Ireland and head to Canada. He left home seeking employment and a promising new life for himself and his family in the New World. Life in this faraway country proved to be a lonely, discouraging existence for him. Sean was homesick for Maggie and his children. He was full of longing for the life he used to lead. Letters were sparse, sometimes arriving two or three at a time after weeks of no word at all. Although the ships ran regularly between England and Canada, ongoing rumours relayed the possibility that the delays were between Ireland and England. The former had become a country ravaged by turmoil. Innumerable disputes were prevalent between landowners and workers. As barns were raided and crops were set afire, neighbours and friends became enemies, suspicious of one another.

Prior to these uprisings, Sean was considered to be a gentleman landowner and farmer because his land was inherited and had been owned by his family for several generations. Similar to the majority of other large landowners, he was an overseer whose property was rented to tenant farmers. Poor crops and political unrest combined to make the prompt payment of the rents impossible. Land taxes were high and rising all the time. Several of Sean's friends and neighbours evicted their non-paying tenants, only to be boycotted by their customers; consequently, many of the products they had grown were left unsold, eventually rotting on tables at the market stalls. Sheer necessity and an innate love of the land, in particular his land, forced Sean to hang on as long as possible.

Many landowners invested their liquidated money into other ventures. Sean knew how to rotate crops successfully and his live-stock were well-bred and healthy, but unfortunately, his enterprising nature failed to pay taxes and feed a large family. His tenants were unable to keep up their rents; however, he felt responsible for their well-being and he didn't have the heart to send them away.

Sean spent many hours in the packinghouses, learning the busi-ness firsthand from Irish bacon curers who were renowned through-out the world. The quality of their product demanded strict attention to both the excellent selection of livestock and the regularity of cure. By the late 1800s, they were beginning to use a liquid brine or pickle solution, instead of salt, to cure the meat. This process allowed the meat to be stored longer without the fear of taint or spoiling, as the product was completely covered by the brine. Seeking to earn extra money during these difficult times, Sean apprenticed himself to one of the famous Irish smoke houses and trained to become a butcher, hoping this might enable him to hold onto his land.

The Irish Land Purchase Act of 1903 gave him a glimmer of hope. This Act facilitated the Conservative policy of handing out money to the Irish peasants and tenants, thus affording them the opportunity to buy out their landlords. After much soul-searching, recognizing the need for change, Sean began negotiations to sell his land. It was a heart-rending situation. He either faced facts or he would watch the land he loved fall into disrepair. It was time to be realistic and practical. He met with his lawyers, drew up a document of sale, and then called a meeting with his lawyers and his tenants. Very quickly, his land was disposed of, with the exception of the house and a few surrounding acres. The tenant owners eagerly accepted the respon-sibility of farming their own land. Free from the responsibility of overseeing acreage he no longer owned, Sean immediately began searching for work elsewhere.

A group of businessmen was building a new meat-packing facil-ity in Scotland. When Sean contacted them, he explained that he'd trained and worked in the Irish curing and packing houses. With that experience, he was eagerly accepted into their new endeavour. They needed his expertise, as well as his money. When he was offered the opportunity to purchase shares in the new business, everything sounded almost too good to be true. Recognizing the state of political confusion in Ireland, Sean decided to invest in the future and join this entrepreneurial group. Maggie agreed with him, realizing their lives and circumstances had already changed dramatically and they had to try something new. They secured a modest home to rent, 'sight unseen.' It would do until the business was up and running successfully, then they would purchase land and a more permanent home.

Throughout the years, their family had occasionally vacationed in Scotland, so they were moving to a familiar place. With a surge of enthusiasm and optimism, they sold the remainder of their Irish holdings, left some of the funds in a bank in Ireland, and headed for Glasgow.

The small house, on the outskirts of the largest city in Scotland, was a far cry from vacationing in a cottage by the sea. Maggie was several months pregnant with their sixth child when they arrived. Used to fresh country air, family close by, and all the indoor and outdoor activities of a farmer's existence, Maggie tried to compensate for these losses. She planted a vegetable garden in the small fenced-in yard located behind the house. Flowers, herbs and vegetables reminded her of home. She taught the older children how to pull weeds, carefully explaining the difference between the fast growing weeds and the plants germinating from the seeds they'd planted so carefully. Their meager budget was stretched to the limit but, with skill and determination, she kept their household running smoothly. Homemade bread, pies, huge pots of soup and stew kept tummies satisfied.

When their baby girl was born, they named her Margaret Elizabeth after her mother, but she was quickly nicknamed Beth. The attending midwife and Maggie became friends. Tricia often arrived with a basket containing fresh eggs, sugar cookies or butter tarts. Sometimes she stayed for a while to assist her friend with the household duties. She taught the older girls to sew. Alicia took to it naturally, and was soon making simple aprons and basic dresses.

Kathleen and Maeve learned to mend socks and knit, but they preferred working in the garden.

The days were busy and long, but they persisted for two years. It was soon obvious to Sean and Maggie that their investment was not paying off. What few savings they'd brought with them were disappearing too quickly. They talked long into the nights about their hopeless situation. The small meat-processing plant in Glasgow simply did not have the working capital to expand enough to keep their prices reasonable and still earn money. The factory was losing ground quickly and finally closed. Once again, changes had to be made.

Sean, Maggie and their family moved back to Ireland. They made arrangements to live with Maggie's brother, who willingly offered them a home. Tom owned and ran a successful mill. Sean, Maggie and their children moved into the grand house with Tom, his wife and their three children. The household was stretched to the limit, but everyone recognized that this was only a temporary arrangement. Sean spent long hours working at the mill and assisting wherever else he was needed around the homestead.

Sean had learned that Canada was a very strong competitor in the food world. The Canadian prairie farmers grew huge crops of grain which they sold to buyers in England. Canada was also very successful in the world-wide bacon and ham business.

After several months, Sean and Maggie agreed that he must leave the family behind, travel to Canada and seek employment there. He took the remaining funds from the final sale of their home, with high hopes of purchasing farmland in Canada, and headed toward a new life.

Chapter
One

In 1908, Sean boarded a ship sailing from Ireland to Canada. The route involved travelling from Ireland to England, then onward to France, picking up passengers and freight along the way. There was an air of expectation and celebration everywhere they docked. Moments of sadness, tears and farewells also took place as passengers boarded the ship while loved ones remained behind. The crowd on the deck cheered with jubilation when the ship finally turned and headed due west, toward their destination. They were on their way! Somewhere across those waters of the Atlantic Ocean was a land called Canada where their dreams could be realized and promises of a new life lay. It was a long, rough passage on that ship, but fortunately, Sean escaped the seasickness that plagued so many.

Shortly after his arrival, he quickly realized that he needed to alter his optimistic plans. Before he followed his dream and searched for a piece of farm property, he needed to earn money, not spend it.

The best security for himself and his family was to find work immediately. Fortunately, because he was a well-trained Irish butcher, he easily found employment at the Davies' meat-packing plant in Montreal.

The adjustment of living in a large city, working long hours and feeling so alone was difficult. He often walked the streets at night, trying to orient himself in his new surroundings. As he walked through the neighourhoods, he could see into the lives of others by catching glimpses of families through the windows he passed. Sean occasionally experienced a sense of oneness, of belonging, as he recalled the gatherings of his own family. Sometimes, these scenes were comforting. At other times, they made him feel discouraged, fearful and very lonely. Every so often, he considered simply running away and heading west, toward the setting sun. He envied the families in those houses. Would he ever see his loved ones again? Not if he ran away! When he felt his heart racing, as panic threatened him, he forced himself to take a few deep breaths until he became calm. Fortunately, he did not succumb to those dark, fearful moments. He turned his back on those houses, quickened his steps and returned to his cheerful boarding house.

Thoughts of the past few years kept flitting through his mind. He wanted to remember the happy times. Deep within, he knew exactly how close he'd come to abandoning Maggie and their children.

As he continued working in Montreal, several of his fellow workers befriended him and he was invited to their homes. Maggie wrote to him and encouraged the older children to write as well. Life became easier as he focused on the present.

Sean's friend and co-worker, Jack, and his wife, Maria, invited Sean for dinner every Sunday. One Sunday, Jack mentioned to Sean that he was busy organizing the sale of his parents' farmhouse. His father had died recently and his mother was moving in with him and Maria. The farmhouse was located on two acres of land outside the city, about half an hour away by horse and carriage, depending on the weather. The original fifty acres had been sold to a neighbouring farmer several years ago. When Sean showed interest, Jack said, "I'm going there next Saturday. Do you want to ride out with me?" Sean accepted his invitation.

Chapter

Two

The two men talked and shared a few stories as they enjoyed the pleasant drive through the countryside the following Saturday. Eventually, they turned into the lane and Jack pointed out the old family homestead. Sean was pleased to see a sturdy looking house, obviously built from the stone so prevalent in the area. Snow still lay on the frozen ground as Jack told him there were six apple trees behind the house. Several other large trees were identified as sugar maples and oaks.

An empty swing hung motionless from a branch, seemingly waiting to be used. A cluster of tall pine trees graced the north and west sides of the house, providing beauty as well as a wind barrier.

Jack pointed toward a winding, frozen area, explaining that it was a stream that passed through the property. He also mentioned that, during the springtime as the snow and ice melted, the stream swelled in size as it raced by on its way to meet a nearby river. Surrounded by scrub and trees, the stream presented Sean with thoughts of ice-skating and picnics.

The large, red barn was welcoming. A quick look inside revealed some machinery, a carriage, and a sleigh. Both looked poised and ready to be filled with laughing children and pulled by a horse. A side wall was neatly filled with shovels, brooms and other tools, hanging on hooks or placed on shelves. Stalls for animals and a pile of hay caught his eye and he noted a ladder, obviously leading to a hayloft high above their heads.

Closing and latching the barn door, Jack commented that when he lived there as a child, they'd had two horses and three cows. Walking toward the house, they passed an empty chicken house and a small shed. Sean thought everything outside seemed to be in good repair as he followed Jack up the front steps onto a wide verandah which ran along the front of the house. Sean had noticed four wooden rockers and a matching swing in the barn, so now he pictured them on this porch.

As Jack unlocked the heavy front door, he told Sean that the house was being sold with the furnishings included. Family members had been encouraged to take any mementos or articles they wanted before the house went up for sale, but most of the large items were still in place.

The front hall led to a dining room on the left and beyond that was the kitchen, with a fireplace. To the right, a large sitting room looked welcoming with a couch, several chairs and a second, open fireplace.

Straight up from the front door, a staircase led to the second story. It had a main hall, four bedrooms and a large linen closet. Behind a closed door, a narrow stairway took them to a high-ceilinged attic. Every window sill throughout the house was wide enough to sit on, due to the depth of the stone walls. The house was modest, not grandiose, but it was certainly roomy enough for his family.

The drive back to Montreal was relaxing, as each man felt satisfied with the day's events. Enroute, Sean decided to purchase the house and property from Jack. He would hire a young couple to help him prepare the house for his family.

Chapter
Three

Several weeks later, Sean was on a train, heading to Halifax to meet Maggie and the children. Upon arrival, he secured lodging at a boarding house. It was clean and spacious, the rates were reasonable and the older couple who owned it were very hospitable. They promptly arranged transportation to and from the dock with a reliable friend of theirs.

After a good night's sleep and a delicious breakfast, Sean stood on the wharf, hoping to get a glimpse of his family. They were actually arriving today! Dressed in his Sunday best, he cut a dashing figure. The crisp white of his starched shirt, the red paisley tie and shining black shoes belied the fact that the perfectly pressed trousers and jacket were well-worn. Only a discerning eye might note the signs of wear. The deep, charcoal background with the narrow, white pinstripes complimented the grey of his eyes. A fedora sat on his head at a jaunty angle as he leaned against one of the lamp-posts that lined the dock.

The ship had arrived hours ago, but regulations required that all immigrants must be checked by both Immigration and Health authorities. Having experienced the process himself, he understood it could be tedious and knew the wait would be long. Nevertheless, he was at the dock early that morning to assure himself the ship had truly arrived.

Mid-morning, Sean walked back to the street where the driver patiently waited with his horse and carriage. The man seemed comfortable in the shade of a huge oak tree. Quite familiar with the situation, he preferred to stay where he was, making sure his horse had food and water. He whiled the time away whittling, resting and chatting with the other drivers.

As he returned to the waiting area on the dock, the loud, frantic barking of dogs caught Sean's attention. He watched with interest as several large kennels holding Irish Wolfhounds were unloaded from the ship. The large animals were in a frenzy, excited to leave the ship, and eager to be set free. Sean noted that some of the dogs were quiet, cowering in the corners of their kennels, terrified by the noisy scene of horses, carriages, men shouting orders and the other barking dogs. Far away from home, the large animals were obviously feeling the effects of a long journey at sea.

Finally, the hold was emptied of its cargo, and the loaded wagons gradually left the wharf. A friendly deckhand used a bullhorn to inform the crowd that the passengers were starting to arrive on the wharf.

In spite of the long, rough passage and the exhausting disembarkation requirements, the immigrants had obviously spruced up for their arrival. Bright scarves, hats, and bits of jewellery added a festive touch to their outfits; however, slowness of step and an overall demeanour of weariness permeated the scene. Eyes flitted here and there, anxiously searching for familiar faces. Soon loving words and calls of welcome mingled with happy tears.

Sean spotted Maggie. It was her! His eyes glistened as she walked toward the gate, the entourage of children clustered around her. Alicia, their eldest daughter, held hands with two of her sisters, Maeve and Kathleen. Frank walked along holding hands with Dorothy. Sean approached his wife, emotion filling his voice as he said, "Maggie!"

God, how he had missed her! Blue eyes connected with grey eyes as tears trickled down their cheeks. He hugged her and the toddler in her arms. Lips lingering on Maggie's for a brief moment, his voice broke as he whispered, "It's been a long time darling, too long."

As he reached out to take Beth in his arms, the child drew back quickly, pressing her face into her mother's shoulder. Maggie smiled. "Give her time, Sean."

Stepping back, he noticed the child's blue eyes watching him. He imagined she was wondering who this man was, kissing her mom. Suddenly, everyone seemed to be hugging him and speaking at the same time. His children had grown and changed during the past two years. Embracing Maggie again, attempting to take the weight of his youngest daughter from her arms, he was spurned again as Beth turned her face, refusing to look at him. He'd truly become a stranger to her.

He guided them to the waiting carriage. The driver loaded them and their belongings on board, then drove the horses away from the wharf toward the rooms Sean had secured. A warm welcome and a hearty dinner awaited them. Two years was a long time to be parted, but finally, they were together.

Chapter Four

Following a good night's sleep and a sumptuous breakfast, they left Halifax, travelling by train to Montreal. The children were excited, as this was their first experience on a train. They watched the changing landscape outside the windows, read and were read to, told each other stories, played games, napped and listened to the eerie, haunting whistle. The motion of the train lulled them to sleep at night.

Frank sketched the lively scenes at the stations whenever the train stopped to leave or pick up passengers. He captured the ever-changing landscape, the farms, thick forests and large bodies of water, but it was people's faces that intrigued him the most. His sketch book quickly filled. Sometimes the train slowed down as they passed through the villages. It was fun to watch the conductor lean way out, holding a letter at the end of a pole while another man stood waiting on the station platform. As the man on the platform deftly grasped the mail, the train gained speed and they continued on their way.

Three days later, they arrived in Montreal. Sean hired a driver with a large carriage, drawn by two horses, to take them home. One by one, the children fell asleep as they left the city behind. Sean was thankful it was spring, as tiny new leaves opening in the sunshine gave the land a hint of green. Close to an hour later, the horses turned into their lane, where the stone house awaited them. Several fruit trees blossomed in shades of pink and white. Here and there, tulips and daffodils nodded a cheery welcome. The breeze carried a hint of lilacs.

Picturing the house and area through Maggie's eyes, Sean knew it was vastly different from their home in Ireland. Would she be disappointed? He doubted it, as the past few years had held many hardships and changes for all of them. At least they'd be together.

As if reading his mind, she reached across and held his hand, blue eyes glistening with a hint of tears. "I'm so happy to be here with you, Sean. Sometimes I wondered if we'd ever be together again. Especially at night, when fear crept into my mind." Brushing the tears from her cheeks, she gave him a brilliant smile. His heart filled with love and admiration.

They wakened the sleeping children. Thankfully, it was still daylight. Soon, everyone was tumbling out of the carriage. Each one carried a satchel to the front porch as Sean, Frank and the driver finished unloading the rest of their luggage. Politely refusing their offer of refreshments, the driver fed and watered his team, waved goodbye and headed back to Montreal.

Meanwhile, the children raced here and there, exploring the house, the barn and the other outbuildings. When Sean opened the house door and called to them, they hurried upstairs, eager to see their sleeping arrangements. Sean placed Maggie's luggage in the room he'd previously claimed for them. It was the largest room, with a window that faced east. The double bed was neatly made, topped with a colourful quilt. Two easy chairs sat by the fireplace. The bedside table held a kerosene lantern and some candles.

The other three rooms were fitted with beds decked out with a variety of lovely quilts. Each bedroom also had a clothes closet, a dresser with a hand-painted pitcher and matching bowl for washing up, and a chair or two.

Sean smiled as Maggie commented on everything he'd prepared for their arrival. "I've enjoyed setting things up, wanting you and the children to feel a sense of being at home."

Alicia and Maeve decided to welcome Beth into their room. With two beds available, she could take turns sleeping in one bed, or the other, with a big sister. Kathleen and Dorothy were pleased to be sharing another room that had two beds. The smallest bedroom was perfect for Frank. An artist's easel stood near a window with northern exposure. Frank was pleased and touched by his father's thoughtfulness.

Everyone seemed content to organize their belongings and settle in. As evening fell, the supper dishes were quickly washed and dried. They were all tired and ready to go to bed. The dusk of evening turned to the black of night and gradually, the excited voices calmed down as sleep overtook them one by one.

Night-time noises could be heard through the open window as crickets chirped and an owl joined the serenade. Maggie sat by the dressing table in her nightgown, brushing her long, dark hair. Sean had dreamt of this moment. He walked over to her and placed his hands on her shoulders. As Maggie's eyes met his in the mirror, she turned her head and kissed his hand. Drawing her up and into his arms, he held her close. They kissed gently, then passionately. Sean extinguished the lantern as they slipped into bed. The room glowed softly, lit by the last glowing embers of the fire. They held each other close as hands tenderly, eagerly explored bodies that seemed fresh and new, yet so familiar. A special touch or kiss on breast or arm and old feelings were aroused. Pleasure soared and brought them to a new awareness of each other. Sated and weary, spent by their passion, they lay quietly side by side. It felt so good, so right to be together again.

Sean sensed by her breathing that Maggie was not yet asleep. He gathered her into his arms and whispered in her ear, "Welcome home, dear one. I feared that you would decide not to follow me here. Ireland has always meant so much to you, Maggie. Ireland and your family. I'd have understood, you know, but I felt so alone without you. I need you. I love you."

Comforted by his warmth and the security of his presence beside her, she snuggled against him, savouring the feeling of him at her back, his arm around her. Communication between them had never been difficult, but tonight, words somehow seemed inadequate to express all the thoughts flying through her mind.

She sighed, saying, "I love you too, Sean. It's as simple as that. Home means being with you. Night after night, I imagined you were beside me by placing a pillow at my back, pretending you were snuggled there." Her voice quivered as she continued, "I know it hasn't been easy for either of us, but we do belong together. You're as much a part of me as my hand, my heart. I have longed to hear your voice reading or reciting to us. We have all missed you."

Chapter
Five

The crowing of a rooster wakened them early the following morning, announcing loud and clear that a new day was beginning. Sean eagerly looked forward to helping Maggie and the children settle in. He had already purchased the seeds for a summer garden and they lay waiting in the shed, ready to be planted when the land warmed up. The hens were laying well. Spring was here and the summer months would allow everyone time to adjust before the school year began in the fall. Thankfully, Sean's job at the meat-packing plant seemed secure. The day dawned with promise.

Summer flew by and the household gradually established a routine. They worked diligently, tending the garden, washing and ironing, cooking and cleaning. Each child was assigned specific chores. Sean and Frank prepared a root cellar, carting containers of sand from the riverbank, packing it into a wooden enclosure they built into a corner of the cellar, and then placing hay around three sides to keep the area insulated. Vegetables, mainly carrots, beets, parsnips and potatoes, were stored beneath the sand, then covered with old newspapers as added protection from the cold winter weather. Beth drew a small map that showed the general position of where each variety was stored and Frank tacked it on a beam nearby.

Maggie and the older girls spent many days preserving apple sauce, peaches, plums, pears, jellies, jams, dill pickles and de-boned chicken pieces in glass jars. Each packed jar was lowered gently into a steaming canner until it held about eight jars, then boiled for a specific length of time, removed and set to cool on the counter. They were later checked to make certain the seals had worked, then the colourful assortment was eventually lined up neatly in their fruit cellar. This cool room was located in the basement under the house. A large, covered clay container sat in a corner, filled to the brim with sweet pickles. After days of preserving, the shelves held a variety of jars, full of mouth-watering foods that would sustain them throughout the winter months.

Life was not all work. There were many glorious hours when they enjoyed the long, lazy days of summer, playing ball and croquet, tag, or hide-and-go-seek. They practiced somersaulting, turning cartwheels and jumping over barriers that Frank constructed for them. On other days, after the cow was milked, the animals fed, the eggs collected and the weeding finished, work was set aside and they'd all head off for a picnic. Their favourite spot was under a large oak tree that stood beside the deepest waters of the stream at the edge of their property. Quilts were spread on the ground and picnic baskets were set in the shade. After swimming, fishing, relaxing and eating, when it was time to head for home, everyone was flushed with sunshine and happiness.

Evenings were special. After dinner, the family usually went outside for a bit of fresh air. After a walk or a few games, they'd gather on the verandah or in their sitting room. Sean often read or recited aloud, while Maggie and the girls busied their hands with knitting, embroidering or mending. Daily troubles, anxieties and quarrels were all forgotten as their father's expressive voice brought magic into the room. A love of reading was instilled in each one of them. Frank's sketch book was always by his side. As the simple home scenes touched him, he'd pick up his pen and effortlessly capture fragments of the moments, knowing he'd paint them at a later date.

Chapter Six

Early in July, Elizabeth McDonald was the guest of honour at a pot luck church supper. She'd been watching Maggie and the children as they bustled around, helping with several jobs.

When she arrived at their table, offering fresh cups of steaming tea, she introduced herself to Maggie.

"Hello. I'm Elizabeth McDonald. I noticed you have a good-sized family. Your children will probably be my students since I'm the teacher at the one room schoolhouse. Would you like to have a tour of the school in a few days? I'm staying at a farmhouse less than a mile from you. I can come to your house and we can walk to the school together."

Maggie eagerly accepted her invitation. A few days later, Elizabeth arrived at their house and the two of them continued on to the school. There was a stale smell as they entered the single classroom. That would soon change when school began. Meanwhile, everything looked fresh and clean. The inside walls had been painted for the new teacher's arrival. Empty wooden desks were lined up in five rows, each one holding six desks. They sat waiting to be occupied, smelling of the thin coat of varnish that had been applied to each one. Within a few weeks, students from the ages of five to thirteen, in kindergarten through to grade eight, would all occupy the same room. It seemed like a challenge to Maggie.

Elizabeth tested a few of the desk drawers, scanned her larger desk at the front of the room, and then picked up a piece of chalk. She wrote 'Maggie' and 'Elizabeth' on the blackboard in strong cursive handwriting, then she rubbed the names out with a brush.

Turning to Maggie, she remarked, "I'll return and check the supplies more thoroughly on another day. I want to empty the supply cupboard and count the pencils, scribblers, ink stands, pens, art supplies and several other things. I will make a list of the extras I will need. Each age group is different, of course, but some basic items will be used by all the students."

Maggie lingered by the book shelves, remarking, "What an impressive variety and number of books, Elizabeth! Perhaps I shouldn't be surprised, but I am."

They entered the cloak room together, noting the sturdy hangers and the pegs on the walls. Elizabeth commented, "Imagine how different this will look, Maggie, when it's filled with all the colourful winter coats, mittens, and scarves."

Both of them noticed that the outer door and the steps leading up to it were in good repair. They smiled at each other as they left. The main door was painted a bright red. Somebody with imagination and a sense of joy had chosen the colour and wielded the paintbrush.

They arrived back home, ready for a cup of tea. The children were pleased to spend some time with their teacher. She made a point of asking each one's name. As Elizabeth was leaving, Maggie invited her to join them for dinner on the following Sunday.

Elizabeth went over the children's names as she followed the path home. Alicia was the eldest. She was petite, with jet-black hair like her mother's. Her skin was white and her dark eyes sparkled when she told Elizabeth she was learning to sew. Maeve was the next one. She had olive skin and chocolate brown hair. Her eyes were large and very blue. Elizabeth thought of the palest shade of hyacinths. Kathleen was next. Her hair and eyes were the hue of a polished chestnut. Elizabeth had heard her singing as she tidied up after tea. Then came Frank. What a handsome boy he was! Black hair like Maggie's, with grey eyes like Sean's. Dorothy was tall for her age, and her fair hair was captured into two braids. Her eyes were also blue, but darker than Maeve's. Beth had curly, strawberry blonde hair. It was tied back with a ribbon, but curls kept springing out. Blue-eyed and rosy-cheeked, she too was a pretty girl. They were all lean and very active. They worked around the house and in the garden, but loved playing ball and running. Elizabeth thought they were delightful, exciting and full of action.

They spent many days together during the rest of the summer, as Elizabeth began assisting Maggie and the children with the chores. She was often a guest at their evening meals. This was the beginning of a lasting friendship.

One evening, toward the end of summer, after the dishes were washed and dried and the table was set for breakfast, everyone went outdoors, as usual. Elizabeth and Maggie sat on the porch, sharing a pot of tea. Sean was in the city, attending a company meeting. Every once in a while, the sharp 'whirrr' of the cicadas broke the silence and the children's voices reached their ears from somewhere near the barn.

Maggie turned toward her friend, saying, "Elizabeth, I don't know what I'd have done without you this summer."

"Thanks for the kind words, Maggie, but I'm certain you'd have managed well enough without me. But I agree, this has been a wonderful summer! Spending time with you, Sean and the children has given me a new purpose in life. I've been so busy I haven't had time to think or to worry."

Maggie's voice was serious as she replied, "All the help you've given us and I realize I've never asked why you came to this country alone? It must have taken great courage!"

Elizabeth responded, "Deciding to move here wasn't a difficult decision. I'm the youngest of thirteen children." With a winsome smile, a touch of sadness crept into her voice as she continued speaking, "Our large farm in England was gradually divided amongst the boys. My two older sisters married well and moved to London where their husbands worked. I was the youngest, so I stayed with my parents, helping around the house. They were killed in a freak carriage accident, coming home in the dark from a neighbour's house. There'd been a lot of rain. While they were visiting their friends, a small bridge was suddenly washed away. On their trip home, the horse, buggy and my parents plunged into the swollen waters. They drowned." She paused for a few moments, remembering that horrendous time.

Then she continued speaking. "It was a shocking, sad time for all of us. My parents were good people. But time moves on. Everything was well-organized, so their estate was settled quite quickly. Most of the land had already been given to the family, so the house was to go to the eldest son, my big brother. He and his wife graciously offered me a permanent home with them, as they planned to move immediately into the house. My parents left me a small allowance. I was young, in my early twenties, and I didn't want to become the spinster aunt so I left home, travelled to Paris and studied to be a teacher. I cleaned houses and worked as a nanny to earn the extra funds I needed. It was simply another challenge, as well as an adventure, for me to come to Canada as a schoolmarm. When I heard that a teaching position was offered here, I applied and was hired. The fact that I speak French fluently helped me find employment. I'm glad to be able to teach in both English and French. Youngsters grasp languages so quickly. Just think how easily yours will learn another language when school begins in a few weeks!"

She hesitated, then continued, "I'm happy here, Maggie. I love being out in the countryside. Teaching is rewarding and working with children, molding impressionable young minds, provides me with a good living and a great feeling of accomplishment."

Maggie contemplated Elizabeth's words. She'd learned a lot about her new friend in the last few minutes and felt selfish for not inquiring about her past weeks ago. How different their lives had been!

Suddenly, the sound of cries and screams broke the peaceful mood. Both women jumped to their feet and hurried toward the noise. Utter chaos reigned as Dorothy and Beth were pelting three weeping children with tomatoes, while they cowered in the garden between the chicken coop and the fence. The targets of their abuse were children from one of the neighbouring farms.

Kathleen was yelling at the top of her voice. "Get off our property, you waifs! You're stupid and dirty! Go home and don't come back!"

Alicia, Frank and Maeve had been sitting in the orchard, taking turns reading aloud to each other, and they arrived on the scene at the same time the two women did.

"Stop that right now!" yelled Maggie. Her startled daughters turned in shock toward their mother and the noise ceased. Kathleen burst into tears and ran toward the house.

Alicia, Elizabeth and Maggie took the neighbour children inside and gently washed the tomato stains from their arms, legs and tear-streaked faces. They soothed their hurt feelings and, half an hour later, they were on their way home, escorted by Frank and Maeve. Each child was happily munching on a butter tart.

After they left, Elizabeth offered to take Beth upstairs and settle her in, as the little girl was upset and crying. Maggie nodded. She planned to seek an explanation from Kathleen, who was still sitting on the porch, refusing to come inside. She couldn't speak without bursting into tears again.

Dorothy was the only culprit left to tell her mother the story. "Mom, we didn't mean to hurt anybody. Kathleen, Beth and I were playing hide-and-go-seek. Kathleen raced off to hide somewhere behind the chicken coop. I guess she surprised herself, and them, as they were sitting in the veggie garden eating tomatoes. We heard the commotion and ran to see what was up. We started throwing tomatoes at them and they tossed some back at us. At first, it was great fun and we all laughed! Then, suddenly, Kathleen got really upset. She started yelling angry words."

Dorothy paused, then spoke again, looking anxiously at her mother, "We didn't mean to hurt them, Mom."

Maggie shook her head sadly. "You must never, ever pick on others like that. And they are so much younger and smaller than you. I'm so sad this happened, but perhaps it will be a good lesson for everyone."

Wondering what to do next, she sent Dorothy up to bed, asking Alicia, Maeve and Frank to go upstairs too, suggesting they get ready for bed and read a few stories aloud to calm everybody down. Elizabeth came downstairs, said goodnight and left for home.

Maggie walked onto the porch and sat down beside Kathleen. The girl was sitting alone, her face buried in her arms.

"Why on earth did you attack those children?" Maggie asked.

Her daughter raised a tear-stained face as her large, brown eyes looked sorrowfully at her mother. Her voice was barely above a whisper when she answered, "I hate peasants like them. It's their fault we had to leave our home in Ireland. They took our place."

Shocked by her daughter's words, Maggie reached for her hand and held it as she answered, "That's not true, my dear. Is that how it seemed to you? It's very difficult for me to explain what happened in Ireland, even to myself. I've thought about it often. Perhaps many of us had too much for too long. Time brought change to the world and to our lives. Come up to bed now. We'll talk more in the morning."

Sean arrived shortly after. He'd had a long day at work. It took time for him to unhitch the horse from the carriage and care for it in the barn. His footsteps were slow as he came upstairs. Maggie decided not to worry him with any talk about the upset.

As she tried to fall asleep, Maggie thought to herself, *I must take more individual time with each of the children.*

Chapter
Seven

The following day, specific chores were assigned, as usual, to the children. It was Kathleen's turn to gather the eggs. As she took the basket and started towards the chicken coop, Maggie called to her. "I haven't done this job for a while, so I'm coming with you and we'll work together this morning."

Silently, they checked inside the coop and found a few eggs, then headed to the haystack in the barn. The chickens often ran free and they seemed to prefer laying their eggs in there. It took a bit more searching to find them.

They'd gathered over a dozen eggs when Kathleen broke the silence. "I really didn't mean to hurt them, Mom. I'm so sorry."

Maggie replied, "I know that, dear, but you've made me realize that your dad and I should have discussed with you what happened back in Ireland and in Scotland. I was so busy planning, working, doing, worrying, and caring for baby Beth at the time, I didn't even think about how you children were feeling. Of course you missed the gardens, horses, picnics and school, but hopefully, we can do some of those things here. We'll build a new life together."

Then she added, "Kathleen, when we get back to the house, I want you to take one dozen eggs and a few other goodies to the O'Malleys. We can prepare the basket together. This will be our way of showing that we care. They are our neighbours and it's about time we started being friendly."

Kathleen was shocked and angrily replied, "We need the eggs. I won't go to their dirty house!" She set the basket on the ground, ran into the house and up the stairs, slamming the bedroom door.

Maggie followed her upstairs, opened the door and walked into the bedroom. "You can and you will, young lady. Come downstairs immediately. Wash your hands and off you go. Take Beth with you. And maybe while you're there, you can both stay and help the poor woman. Ten children, all under twelve, and I think I'm busy!"

Her mother's mouth was firm and her eyes were snapping. Kathleen opened her mouth to answer back, then closed it with a resigned set to her jaw. She knew she'd probably gotten off easy. She grudgingly helped her mother prepare the gift basket, then left with Beth in tow to visit their neighbours.

That afternoon, Maggie gathered the children around her. It was time she explained a few things to them. She had asked Elizabeth to be present. Maggie's heart filled with love as she looked at them.

Praying her words would help, she began speaking. "It isn't fair that some people are wealthy, while others have barely enough to live on. Your father, grandfather and other ancestors worked diligently to oversee their land. They also cared about their tenants and treated them fairly. It was not the same everywhere. Some landowners took from the land and the people. They pursued wealth and pleasure at the expense of others. We all paid for their lack of perception and forethought."

She paused to gather her thoughts, then continued. "When troubled times came, your father and I had serious decisions to make. We sought other opportunities. Moving to Scotland, your dad worked hard, but that business went under. We lost money. Returning to Ireland was our only choice, given the circumstances. We were fortunate to be welcomed into your Uncle Tom and Aunt Irene's home in Ireland. Your father moved here to Canada to seek work, earn some money and prepare for us. Life has not been easy for any of us, but especially for him."

She planned her next words carefully, saying, "Now I want to discuss what happened here yesterday. Regardless of what occurs in your lives, I want you to remember that no human being is better than another. Regardless of colour, beliefs, religion, wealth, poverty, talents, hopes and dreams, we are all human beings. Humans who just happened to be born on this planet Earth. No child can choose his parents, or where he or she is born. Wars are fought because of these differences. When we learn to respect and at least try to understand others, we become stronger. Your father and I want each one of you to study diligently and get an education. Someday, you'll be in a position to make your own way in life. By respecting yourself and other human beings, you will understand that they have as much right to live on this earth as you do. Most importantly, always remember that I love you."

As the weeks passed, Kathleen often asked her mother's permission to visit the O'Malleys. She enjoyed telling the children stories and singing to them. Their household was very busy, but it was kept as clean as possible. Boots and shoes were lined up neatly by the back door, as the family members were not allowed to walk in with muddy footwear. There was always something delicious cooking in a pot on the stove or baking in the oven. The O'Malleys loved listening to 'their Kathleen' sing at church services.

Chapter
Eight

Summer slipped by, and the school year was scheduled to begin soon. When her landlords decided to put their farmhouse up for sale, Elizabeth began searching for somewhere else to stay.

Knowing her situation, Maggie and Sean decided to offer the third floor of their home to Elizabeth. It was an attic that was used for storage, but the floor was solid wood. Although the slanted ceiling followed the shape of the roofline, it was high enough to enable a tall person to walk safely around without bumping a careless head. Two windows allowed light and fresh air into the area.

The room held boxes of articles that could be safely stored in the barn. Soon it was emptied, scrubbed clean, windows polished and freed of spider webs. The next day, Maggie took Elizabeth upstairs, showed her the new room and offered it to her. She was delighted! Within a week, Sean and Frank had moved her few belongings from the farmhouse into her new suite. It held her bed, dresser, desk, a couple of chairs, and a cedar chest, with lots of room to spare. Elizabeth purchased a used piano that was for sale in the neighbourhood and Sean, Frank, and a couple of other men moved it into their parlour. Everyone was delighted as music filled their home again.

Elizabeth's arrival into their home proved to be a perfect situation, as she and Maggie were good company for one another. They also knew that, when the winter months arrived, the snowy weather would often force Sean to stay in Montreal during the week. Initially, Elizabeth's offer to pay rent was refused, but when she told them the school board was obligated to pay for her accommodations, they accepted. As a gesture of appreciation for the lovely, private area, Elizabeth insisted on purchasing a few groceries. She also continued assisting the children with their homework and helping around the house.

Autumn turned the leaves to brilliant colours of red, orange and gold. When they loosened and fell to the ground, the children had a wonderful time raking, piling, jumping and playing in them. Eventually, the remnants that didn't blow away with the wind were carted to a compost heap behind the barn. Sweaters were replaced by hats and coats.

As winter approached, Sean was very busy at the packing plant. Rumours regarding the terrible sanitary conditions in many food processing plants caused great concern for the owners. Government inspectors often arrived unexpectedly to check the working conditions. As one of the foremen, Sean tried to instill a sense of 'pride of product' in the people who worked under him. He paid attention to the general cleanliness of the workers, as well as the premises. This added longer hours to his already lengthy days. During the spring and summer, he had enjoyed his daily trips back and forth to Montreal, often remarking to Maggie, "I do my best planning on those buggy-rides!"

As the days grew shorter and darkness fell earlier, the trip was not as tolerable. During his first winter there, a fellow worker had offered Sean a place to stay in his family's home when the weather was bad. Discussing this with Maggie, they mutually decided that it was a wise move. He was able to return home unless a violent snow storm hit. It was a comfort for Maggie, knowing that he wasn't attempting to travel during those times.

Beth sometimes wished she could go to school with the others, but she knew that five was the magic number. That special birthday wouldn't happen until next year because she'd only turned four in June. Most mornings, she enjoyed dusting, drying dishes, sampling cookies, licking beaters and helping her mother tidy up.

This was a very special day! Last night, while she was tucked in bed sleeping, Alicia, Elizabeth and Maggie had chopped and prepared the mixture of fruit and nuts for the Christmas cake. Beth sat at the table, watching as her mom measured the flour and seasonings, beat the butter, slowly added the sugar and the eggs, and then put everything together. Maggie stirred the whole marvellous concoction with a large wooden spoon until everything was well mixed. Then, cup by cup, the batter was put into the prepared pans and placed in the oven to bake. They tidied the kitchen together, then Maggie looked at her and said, "Beth, let's go outside for a walk. The fresh air will feel good."

Putting on hats and coats, scarves, mittens and boots, mother and daughter walked out the door into a snowy wonderland. The sun felt warm on their faces, though the air was crisp and bitterly cold. Maggie bent over to pull Beth's scarf up to protect her cheeks from the frosty air. The regal evergreens were heavy with the new snow that had fallen during the night. Every once in a while, a gentle puff of wind caused their heavily laden branches to shake and toss a clump of snow onto the ground with a 'plop.' They followed the lane, stopping to watch a chickadee as it flitted through the yard searching for food.

Along the sunny side of the barn, some chickens busily scratched, discovering a few seeds on the ground below the tall, frozen sunflower stalks that stood with drooping heads. Maggie told Beth that many of the summer birds travelled far away to spend the cold winter months in southern countries, then they'd fly back to their northern homes during the warmth of spring.

The comforting aroma of Christmas spices greeted them as they returned from their walk. Soon they were sitting together, sharing their usual mid-morning tea party, while Beth's rag doll, Amy, sat and watched.

Chapter
Nine

In the following year, Beth turned five and was pleased that she was finally old enough to attend school. During her first year, at 'recitation time,' Beth stood up and recited the entire poem of Hiawatha in front of all the students. Everyone applauded as she sat back down.

The children eagerly sang their sister's praises when they arrived home from school that day. Dorothy was the first one to call out. "Mom! You should have heard Beth! She did a really good job of saying her poem!"

That evening, Elizabeth turned toward Maggie as they sat knitting. "It's good to hear the children praise Beth. They are very proud of their little sister. Your shy, youngest daughter has an amazing ability to memorize. She recited Hiawatha perfectly, from beginning to end, surprising everyone! Maggie, it was her expression and delivery that amazed me. That poem came alive, just as it does when Sean recites or reads aloud to us. She has a natural gift."

Maggie smiled and nodded. "Beth has listened to Sean recite that poem since she was a baby. They were apart a couple of years, but he's continued reading and reciting since we arrived. He'll be pleased to hear that Beth found the courage to recite it at school. Your individual attention with schoolwork and everything else has helped them all, Elizabeth. You've spent so much time with each one. Everything might have been very different around here without your help."

Appreciating the comments, Elizabeth replied, "They also help each other. You and Sean are great parents."

That night, Maggie lay in bed thinking about her children. They were all excellent students. Their days were active as they learned to cook and bake, as well as helping with other chores at home. Regardless of their 'togetherness,' they were such individuals! Each child seemed to have at least one unique talent. Alicia baked, gardened and sewed like a professional seamstress. Maeve was always writing stories and poems, with dreams of becoming a nurse. Kathleen excelled at playing the piano and sang like an angel. Frank was good at most things, but he was their artist, always drawing or painting. And Dorothy, well, Dorothy was an entertainer. She raced with the wind and danced to any tune. Everyone enjoyed her spontaneity and eagerly participated in her 'make-believe' plays. Beth wanted to be a teacher, like Elizabeth. Reading was a common family enjoyment. Whenever there was spare time, they could be found with their 'noses in a book.' In spite of life's traumas and changes, their family seemed to be thriving.

The grandfather clock that Sean had brought home faithfully ticked the hours away as another Christmas approached. Where had the time gone? They'd had several snowfalls, so Sean stayed in Montreal often, coming home on the weekends whenever possible. Elizabeth and Maggie sat at the kitchen table, chopping dates and apricots, measuring raisins, cherries and nuts for the traditional Christmas fruitcake. This pleasant chore was one they both looked forward to sharing. As they chatted, Maggie revealed the fact that she was expecting another child in the spring. Opening her mouth to congratulate Maggie, Elizabeth paused, sensing the gravity of her friend's voice and noting her troubled eyes.

She listened quietly as Maggie spoke. "I'm afraid, Elizabeth. The prospect of a new baby usually makes me feel so happy and fulfilled, but this time my emotions are mixed. I'm not as young as I used to be. Sadly, I feel different, almost guilty about bringing another child into our family. Sean and I have had our hands full these past few years and now we've settled into a good routine. Throughout the years, our lives have changed significantly. We've both been tested mentally, physically and spiritually. My enthusiasm for another child is simply non-existent."

She sighed, then continued, "With thoughts like these, I don't even know myself anymore and I'm afraid of this stranger in my head. Sometimes, I waken early in the morning feeling lost and out of place."

Elizabeth simply reached for Maggie's hands and held them. "Please remember I'm here with you and will help however I can. Lean on me when you need to. It seems wrong for me to be measuring raisins and blithely say that 'everything will be all right' and 'don't worry.' They are just words. I often wonder how you cope with everything so well and I can't even imagine the stress you've been through. The wise ones say 'one day at a time,' and perhaps they're right. That's all any of us have."

Neither woman spoke as they finished the preparations for the cake, covered the bowls and placed them in the pantry. When the job was finished, Elizabeth hugged Maggie and they headed upstairs.

Moonlight peeked through her bedroom window as Elizabeth knelt and said her prayers. With tear-filled eyes, she climbed alone into her cozy bed, feeling worried about her friend. Before drifting off to sleep, she whispered aloud, "Perhaps, when tomorrow comes and the ingredients are all combined, spooned into the baking tins and placed in the oven to bake, the spicy aroma of Christmas floating through the air once more will lighten Maggie's heart."

Meanwhile, Maggie brushed her hair, braided it loosely and prepared for bed. She felt better after talking with Elizabeth. The time had come to share her news with Sean. She realized that he probably suspected she was pregnant. Perhaps he was waiting for her to say something as she'd usually been eager to share such news with him. A few weeks ago, he'd commented that she'd lost weight and hoped she wasn't working too hard.

Meanwhile, either work or weather held him in Montreal most week nights, and on the few days he was home, their busy household kept them both occupied. Most nights, they just headed upstairs exhausted and ready to sleep.

The following Sunday, Maggie told Sean her news. He'd watched her with anxious eyes recently, as her usual liveliness and sparkle seemed to leave her, so he was not surprised. That evening, he listened, holding her in his arms for a few minutes before speaking.

"It hurts me to see you suffer, Maggie. Knowing you were barely eating anything, I kept thinking you had a 'touch' of something. Last weekend, I suspected the truth. I know you so well. Your eyes seemed troubled and I sensed your fears. It's not the best time for either of us, is it? Of course, we'll welcome the new little one, but I hope you feel better soon."

He snuggled up to her back, spoon-fashion, and they fell asleep.

Chapter
Ten

Monday evening, Elizabeth and Maggie sat together at the kitchen table, busily wrapping the cooled Christmas cakes in brandy soaked cheese cloth, then in wax paper, and placing them into special storage tins. They carried the delectable packages into the pantry, lined them up on a shelf, and then smiled at each other with satisfaction.

Maggie said, "Now I feel that Christmas is really on its way."

Elizabeth nodded her head in agreement, saying "You have such a beautiful family. I do envy you that. Another baby probably seems like an added burden right now, but please let me help as much as possible. I've never had much experience around babies, but I'm sure I can learn!"

Maggie laughed. "You are such a delight to have around! Trust me, your help is always appreciated. I told Sean about the baby last night. Sharing with you both has cheered me up."

As Christmas drew closer, the severe bouts of nausea eased, Maggie felt better and her appetite improved. She tired easily, as her strength and energy seemed to be flowing right through her to the child growing within. She learned to give in to her weariness and made a point of relaxing and sitting down more often. She and Elizabeth continued walking outside after dinner. They would only walk for fifteen minutes or so, but the cool night air agreed with them both. They'd return home rosy-cheeked and happy. Elizabeth, Kathleen and Maggie took turns playing the piano, and everyone gathered round to sing Christmas carols.

When school was let out for the holidays, the children spent several evenings at the church, practicing for the annual Christmas concert. Buggies lined up as families arrived from all the neighbouring farms, turning the concert rehearsals into a welcome social event. The church kitchen was a busy place where the women prepared treats of hot cocoa and tea for everyone. The parents brought a variety of goodies for all to share. Alicia usually preferred to stay at home, but this year, Elizabeth encouraged her to participate by insisting that she needed her help with the younger children. Alicia eagerly joined the festivities.

On Christmas Eve, the pungent scent of pine greeted everyone as they entered the church. A tall spruce tree, complete with lighted candles, stood proudly near the altar. The congregation was invited to join in with the choir as they sang the familiar carols prior to the service.

During the evening, several children of various ages recited or read verses appropriate for the occasion. The living Nativity scene was enacted by students portraying Mary, Joseph, the Christ child, the three Wise Men and the Shepherds. Two sheep were brought in, but they were hurriedly taken back outside when their bleating drowned out the children's voices. Everybody laughed as they were led back down the aisle. Specific verses from the Bible were read as the beautiful Christmas story unfolded before their eyes.

The service ended when Kathleen moved to the front of the choir and sang 'O Holy Night.' There was scarcely a dry eye in the church as her glorious voice soared through the air. The final treat was when the minister stood at the door, handing out hard candies and oranges to each child, wishing all a Merry Christmas.

Christmas Day dawned bright and crystal clear. Gifts were exchanged, with as much pleasure felt in the giving as in the receiving. Handmade mittens, scarves, socks and cozy sweaters were always welcome. Alicia was clever at shortening and remaking her sisters' dresses to fit Beth. A set of different buttons or a bit of lace gave each outfit a different look. The little girl was always pleased with her re-made hand-me-downs. This year, she was thrilled to open her gift from Alicia and discover that her sister had designed and sewn a brand new, blue velvet dress for her! It was trimmed with a detachable white collar and cuffs. Tucked inside was a matching outfit for her doll!

After the gifts were exchanged, they sat down to a sumptuous turkey lunch with all the trimmings. Sean felt the sting of tears in his eyes as he watched them all joining hands and bowing their heads to pray. His husky voice asked for God's blessing on their food, and gave thanks for the fact they were healthy and together. The solemn moment passed and they were soon eating with enthusiasm.

During their first winter in Canada, Sean had purchased several pairs of second-hand ice skates. He'd considered waiting for Christmas Day to give them to his family, but had decided that fresh air and exercise would relieve the excess energy that gripped the household during the pre-Christmas days. After lunch, everyone bundled up and headed outside to enjoy the crisp, sunny day. Frank and his sisters shovelled the snow off a large area of the nearby creek so the family could skate. It was such fun!

Later that evening, darkness found them all gathered in the parlour, sitting by the cheery fireplace, sipping hot apple cider and munching on decorated ginger and sugar cookies. Kathleen sang a few songs, accompanied on the piano by Elizabeth. They all joined in the singing and harmonizing as the familiar carols rang through the house. Sean ended the evening by reading aloud.

Long after the others had gone to bed, he sat staring into the glowing embers. Lately, his mind had reeled with plans for the future. He longed to own a large parcel of land and to be his 'own man' again. For the present, he was grateful to be employed and knew in his heart that raising a family required him to keep working and living day by day. He felt content tonight. At least they were together. He bent down and pushed the burnt remnants of a log back into the fireplace. Enough daydreaming.

Chapter
Eleven

Life changed a few weeks later. In January, a typhoid fever epidemic hit Montreal with a vengeance. Each day brought news of more people being stricken with the illness. The city was in a panic as houses, businesses and restaurants were scoured, trying to end the spreading scourge. As the news of more deaths spread, they began closing their doors. Following suit, the meat-packing company was also shut down. Sean planned to head home.

The night before he was to leave, Sean wakened with a severe nosebleed. Within a few hours, he was taken to the hospital in Montreal and placed in an isolated section that was prepared specifically to care for victims of the fever.

Eventually, investigators discovered that this particular breakout of typhoid fever had been caused by contaminated drinking water. It was common practice for groups of men to cut huge blocks of ice from the frozen waters during the winter months. These blocks were stored under sawdust in icehouses to provide refrigeration for ice boxes in homes and for storage houses to preserve food products. These frozen blocks were supposed to be cut from specific areas in the river, well above the flow of water that eventually travelled through the city. It was believed that shysters, eager to make an extra dollar, often cut ice below the city, where the waters of the St. Lawrence River were contaminated by raw sewage. These blocks of ice were sold to unsuspecting clients. As the ice melted on food, or in beverages, the pollutants in the water were widespread.

It was a sad time for everyone, as many people died. Sean remained in the hospital, where he was treated for a month. He returned home with strict orders from his doctor to rest, rebuild his strength, and stay away from his workplace. The business was shut down, so that was no problem.

When Maeve came down with the fever too, Maggie took care of her at home, isolating them both in one of the bedrooms. The girls took turns leaving trays of food on the floor outside the bedroom door. Sean slowly regained his strength as his health improved. Hour after hour, Maggie stayed by her daughter's bedside, bathing her fever-racked body with cool water. The shadows grew darker under Maggie's lovely eyes and her high cheekbones became more prominent as she stubbornly refused to give in to her exhaustion. Finally, Maeve's fever broke and she slowly recovered. The rest of their household members stayed well, miraculously escaping the deadly outbreak. Maggie was thankful that she'd been able to stay strong enough to help out when her family needed her.

There was no income, other than Elizabeth's rent. They almost felt guilty accepting it, as her ongoing assistance was a gift. She continued working with the children, lending her helping hands wherever needed. Fortunately, the preserves they'd laid away, the vegetables stored in the root cellar, and eggs from the chickens, kept food on the table. Occasionally, there was a chicken dinner.

The balance of the money Sean had brought to Canada, from the final sale of their property in Ireland, had been used to purchase their house. In desperation, Maggie wrote to a distant relative who lived in New York. The man had connected with them while on a business trip to Montreal. At that time, he'd asked them to contact him if they ever needed any help getting settled in. Maggie's note briefly explained their circumstances. He provided them with some funds in exchange for their family silver and a few other items of value. It was difficult to part with those items, but they were desperate. Maggie kept the silver napkin holders that were engraved with each child's name. These were the last tangible reminders of their life in Ireland.

Chapter Twelve

On the first day of March, Maggie's labour began, one month earlier than expected. The midwife, who lived nearby, arrived at their house to assist with the birth. For two seemingly endless days, it was debatable whether either the mother or the baby would survive, but in the wee hours of the morning, a tiny baby girl was born. When the newborn was gently placed in her arms, Maggie's heart filled with love for the wee girl. She drifted off to sleep, believing everything would work out well. They named her Muriel Ann, after a friend in Ireland. Following the midwife's suggestion, Maggie and Muriel were moved into a special nursing home for mothers and babies in Montreal, and a wet nurse was brought in to feed the baby. This proved to be a wise decision, as Maggie's recovery was slow and she needed rest.

Muriel had a good appetite and a lusty cry. Initially, she'd caused some worry, as her slow passage through the birth canal, and the final use of forceps to facilitate her birth, had left her head quite marked and malformed. After a few days, the baby looked much better as her head creases gradually reshaped and the marks faded.

When the two weeks were up, Maggie was finally able to leave her bed and sit in a chair for a few minutes each day. It was suggested that she'd be wise to stay another week, but that night, as she rocked Muriel in her arms, she decided that it was time to return home.

Muriel died during the night. The nurse, wondering why the baby wasn't wakening for her feeding, quietly entered the room to check. As she picked her up, she realized that Muriel was lifeless, and she cried out for help, but nothing could be done.

Maggie was heart-broken. A private family service was held in the cemetery behind the church. As the tiny oak coffin was blessed and lowered into the ground, the minister, Maggie, Sean, Elizabeth, the midwife and all the children stood together to say goodbye to the baby. It was a scene that would never be forgotten. The children were pleased to have their mother back home, but her homecoming brought sadness. Whenever they thought about the little sister they would never know, their hearts ached.

Elizabeth had managed the household well during Maggie's absence, calmly directing the younger children to assist Alicia and herself with innumerable jobs. If anyone procrastinated, a quick appeal to Frank usually got the desired effect. He could coax his beloved sisters to do almost anything he asked, even work.

Life slowly returned to normal.

One Saturday morning, Alicia rose early to begin baking. She had often watched her mother make bread, and they had prepared it together a few times. She confidently punched down the initial rising of the dough, allowed it to rest, then rise again before kneading it the final time and shaping it into loaves. Beth was standing on a chair beside her, shaping a small portion of dough into her very own little loaf. Eventually, ten regular loaves and one small one were set on the counter. Alicia pierced each loaf with three diagonal slashes, then covered them with slightly dampened tea towels, allowing them to begin rising once more.

"How long will it take before we can put them in the oven?" asked Beth.

"About an hour, love," replied Alicia. "I'll put more wood on to make sure the oven is hot enough, then we'll go upstairs and look over those dresses I'm altering for you. That's better than standing here watching and waiting for the bread to rise." She opened the fire box as she spoke and added two more logs before they headed up the stairs.

Sewing was Alicia's favourite occupation. She had a natural eye for design. Her sewing skills were noted and sought after by each member of the family. Once again, Beth had outgrown many of her warm weather dresses. Funds were scarce, so Alicia was busy re-making two dresses for her. The green one had belonged to Dorothy, the blue one to Maeve. Alicia tried them on Beth, then asked her to stand on a chair while she marked and pinned the hems. Carrying the dresses, needle and thread, she walked into her mother's room, where Maggie was knitting. As they chatted, neither of them noticed Beth slip out of the room.

After a while, Alicia returned to the kitchen to bake the bread. She was surprised to see that eight loaves were puffing up over the top of the tins while the remaining two loaves and one tiny loaf looked suspiciously flat. "Beth, where are you? Did you touch the bread?"

A very shame-faced Beth walked into the kitchen. "Oh, Alicia, I was just checking them! What happened? Did I ruin them?"

Alicia was annoyed, but knowing Beth well, she realized the deed was truly not an intentional misdemeanour. Skillfully moving the perfect loaves into the oven to bake, she patiently explained what had happened. "The holes you made let the air escape, Beth. I'm just thankful that you at least left these other loaves untouched!"

Alicia decided to leave the three deflated loaves out on the counter longer to see if they would rise any further. They didn't, as the yeast had already outdone itself, but she baked them after the other loaves were done. Beth made a face as she tasted 'first-hand' the difference between successful and unsuccessful bread. The sparrows certainly enjoyed the treat as Beth spread the crumbled, ruined loaves around the backyard.

Fortunately, the city was returning to normal after the epidemic. Businesses re-opened and Sean was feeling strong enough to begin working part-time. He still worried about Maggie, as she was often withdrawn and quiet, but he understood. Thoughts of their baby, the daughter he'd never tell stories to, or rock in his arms, tugged at his heart too.

Chapter
Thirteen

The new year arrived with high expectations and a few surprises. Maggie's brother, Thomas, sent a letter informing them that he, his wife, Irene, and their three children were leaving Ireland and coming to live in Canada. He'd accepted a job offer from James Morris, a family friend, who needed an experienced manager to update a mill in the outskirts of Toronto! The job entailed hiring men to do the repairs necessary to get the mill up and running. Tom sounded excited about the prospects of tackling this new challenge.

"We will be leaving Southampton on April 10, 1912, travelling on the Titanic. We will be docking in New York, then we'll be heading for Canada. It is the fancy ship you have perhaps been reading about. We are, of course, travelling as immigrants. A friend of mine helped us secure passage…"

With mounting excitement, the family read any news they could get hold of regarding the 'largest ship in the world'. The Titanic was 883 feet long. She had 'unsinkable' bulkheads and was supposed to be the most luxurious of the so-called floating hotels.

April brought winter's last hurrah to Montreal with an overnight snowfall of ten inches to herald the new month. On April 14th, the Titanic hit an iceberg. There had been no specific drills to check the crew out on emergency procedures in the event of a tragedy. Many wealthy socialites clung to the upper decks. Confusion reigned.

Some lifeboats left the ship before they were filled. Water flooded six of the ship's water-tight compartments and she sank in the early hours of the next morning. Close to a thousand passengers were rescued, but hundreds of immigrants were trapped below. One thousand five hundred and two people went down with the ship.

As the lists of survivors were published, the family's hopes slowly dimmed. It was almost a certainty that Thomas, Irene and their family had perished in the cold waters of the Atlantic.

Maggie was devastated. Overcome by sorrow, her already weakened condition caused her to go into shock. Not a tear was shed. At first, Elizabeth thought Maggie was simply being stoic, but as days passed, there was no improvement. Maggie gradually ceased speaking at all as she blocked out the world. Occasionally, they'd hear her voice call out in her sleep. If Sean was home, he'd gently hold her trembling body until she fell into a quiet sleep once more.

One day, a letter arrived from James, informing Sean that he was still looking for someone to manage the mill and asking Sean if he would consider taking on that responsibility. In Ireland, Sean had worked at the Kilpatricks' mill, helping to unload the wagons full of grain. After the grain was ground into flour, he helped bag and load the flour which was then sent off to be used in bread, baked goods and cereal products. He understood the business quite well and felt confident that, with skilled help, he could manage the place. His past experiences, working with and guiding other men, would certainly be useful. Surely there were men living near the Applewood Mill who might consider returning to their old jobs. Sean decided to go to Toronto to talk with James. He packed his suitcase and boarded a train in Montreal.

Travelling westward toward Toronto, thoughts and memories flicked through his mind. He was still worried about Maggie. She was herself for a while, then more and more often, since the tragic deaths of her brother and his family, she seemed to be slipping silently away from them. What was going to happen? He couldn't help comparing this silent woman with the lively, young lady he'd met at a county ball in Ireland.

He had fallen for Maggie at that first dance. She was so full of life and obviously well-read, with a sense of mischief and fun that made him laugh. She had delighted in telling him that she was a descendant of the 'disinherited side' of the Hamilton family, entertaining him with family stories and rumours.

Years ago, her grandmother had met and married William Kilpatrick. Unfortunately, her family, the Hamiltons, refused to give the couple their blessing, convinced as they were that it was beneath their daughter to marry a tradesman. She agreed to marry James, in spite of their feelings, fearlessly disregarding their threats and disapproval. The young couple eloped. Because of her rebellion, she was ostracized. Her name was stricken from her father's will and her family literally disowned her.

She became a Kilpatrick and was proud to do so. They were honest, intelligent, hard-working people. Their mill was efficiently managed and run. Respect grew with their ongoing success and excellent reputation. Throughout the years, their business expanded. Sean had felt proud when he married this feisty woman's descendant. Thinking about and remembering those happy times, Sean hoped and prayed that his beloved wife would recuperate soon.

Chapter
Fourteen

When Sean arrived at Applewood Mill, he was greeted by James. He was a short, stocky, pleasant-looking man, with a round face that flashed deep dimples when he smiled. Twinkling eyes revealed his innate sense of humour which affected everyone who came near him. His neighbours were often endowed with gifts of flowers from his garden, fruit from the orchard or wine from the wine cellar. James preferred to spend his time working in the grounds around the lovely estate; the gardens and orchard were well cared for.

Unfortunately, he rarely visited the mill. The men he'd hired to trim the trees and keep the weeds cut down lacked direction, so they took advantage of his good humour and lax attitude toward that property. James was delighted with the prospect of Sean taking over the duties of management. Someone was needed to reform and revitalize the potentially promising business. His banker had informed him that the past owners had run "a very lackadaisical operation," and he stressed that the mill needed immediate attention, or it should be sold.

James had already spoken with several former employees of the mill. They explained that, when their demands for safety improvements were ignored, they left and did not return. The mill was not safe. James related this state of affairs to Sean as they walked down the lane.

The main house was a different matter altogether. Sean was guided up a stone walkway, elegantly bordered with immaculately trimmed hedges. A haze of green met his eyes as tiny, new leaves covered the trees, encouraged by the warmth of the sun. Before them stood a lovely, gracious home. The front entrance opened to shining floors, elegant rugs and impeccable furnishings.

There was no neglect in evidence here. The front hall led to a large drawing room, where a grand piano graced one end. Through French doors on the opposite side of the hall, there was a large library. The formal dining room, kitchen, pantry and breakfast room were at the back of the house. A wide stairway in the front hall curved gently to the upper story where there were five large bedrooms. Each room had ample closets and a fireplace, while the two largest rooms connected to walk-in dressing rooms. At the back of the house, a small narrow stairway led from the kitchen to the bedroom area. This set of stairs also continued on, up to the attic.

"Sean, if you decide to accept the position, this house is yours to live in. I have renovated the guest house for myself. Other than sharing the occasional meal with your family, I'll spend my time there and in the gardens. I'm a quiet man. My happiness is found in a good meal, a bottle of wine, an hour or two in my garden, a leisurely walk, a book, and a visit with friends. I'll be pleased to see this wonderful place inhabited by a family."

As James toured Sean through the house, he related several anecdotes about the previous owners and their servants. He proudly detailed the renovations he had planned and overseen, stressing that he strived to maintain the house in excellent repair, without changing the architecture in any way. It was obvious that he had lavishly spent money on the house.

"In some ways, I've been a real disappointment to my father. He wanted me to be a miller, or at least a businessman capable of overseeing this place. The mill needs strong management. I am simply no judge of workmen and business is not my strong point. We need you, Sean. I've heard that you were highly respected by your tenants at Brookhill. A stiff master, but a fair one. If you decide to come, I have a contract already drawn up for you. My lawyer prepared it when we sent for Thomas. Read over the contract and see if it suits you."

Sean was in a daze as they walked through the house. It was almost beyond comprehension to think that he, Maggie and their children could soon be living in a house like Applewood. He turned to his host and replied, "James, I don't have to think about it. If you will have us, we'll come. Usually I'd discuss this with Maggie, but she is still suffering from the loss of our baby and her brother. Perhaps the change will be good for her and for the children. I don't need to tell you that times have been rough. I can't promise you any miracles, but to the best of my ability, I will proceed with the repairs on the mill. There are many men looking for work. It will take a lot of time and many interviews to hire a strong, knowledgeable work-force, but I believe it is possible. We can talk business immediately, if you so desire."

"Tomorrow, Sean, tomorrow", said James. "First, I want to take you over to my home, where a feast has been prepared for us by my housekeeper. Two of my friends will be joining us for dinner. You'll be staying in my guest room until you return to Montreal. Come along, the men are arriving soon. You have enough time to refresh yourself."

They left the large house and walked through the garden on the south side of the house. Sean noted that a large porch ran across the front of the building. As they passed it, James mentioned that wicker furniture had been stored for the winter and was being repainted. Everything would be in place when the family arrived. They skirted an apple orchard of eight trees as they walked toward a small, stone house located at the back of the gardens. A welcoming curl of smoke rose from the chimney, and the smell of wood-smoke drifted through the air. Sean breathed deeply. He felt at home and peaceful.

Sean stayed for two nights and then returned home, excited to share his news.

He told Maggie first as they sat together in their bedroom before dinner. She sat with her head down as he spoke and he wondered if she was listening.

When he stopped talking, Maggie patted his arm and said, "I'm happy for you. Are we all moving there?"

A doctor in Montreal had told Sean that the longer Maggie stayed withdrawn from everyone, the less chance she had of ever speaking again. Her whole world had shifted inward. He had also mentioned that perhaps she'd have more healing opportunities in one of the mental clinics or hospitals. Sean was reluctant to do that yet. For a few moments, he doubted his spontaneous decision, but he believed it was for the best.

Chapter
Fifteen

As the school year drew to a close, it became apparent that, even with all the changes and adjustments throughout the past few years, the academic achievements of the children had not suffered.

Alicia was burdened with the chore of helping to manage the household, but her bright mind accepted the challenge. She wrote her exams and was awarded a medal for the highest grades in the area. Maeve captured the English honours. The rest of the children received high marks, succeeding in spite of their mother's illness and the extra responsibilities at home. Sean was proud of them.

He was also thankful for Elizabeth, their stalwart friend, helper and teacher. He recognized that, when they moved to Ontario, leaving her behind was not going to be easy for anyone.

Elizabeth continued spending time with Maggie each day. Sometimes, she wondered if another move would have positive or negative results. Maggie's body appeared to be stronger, but her spirit still seemed lost and broken. Her few spoken words were brief. Occasionally, Elizabeth glimpsed a spark of life in those blue eyes. Elizabeth knew they'd miss each other terribly.

The following weeks brought a flurry of activity as the packing was completed and the house was cleaned in preparation for the new owners. Fortunately, they'd also purchased the horse and the other livestock.

When Sean locked the doors for the final time, he drew Elizabeth aside, saying, "Elizabeth, you are part of our family. I can't thank you enough for everything you've done for us. Please come to visit as soon as possible. Perhaps our new location in Ontario will appeal to you. Remember, you'll always have a home with us."

With those parting words, the family gathered round her with farewells and hugs. They were headed for Ontario!

Chapter
Sixteen

Their arrival at Applewood was a joyful one. Exclamations of delight rang through the air as they explored the house and gardens. The warm June days had encouraged the roses to bloom and the colourful flowers sent a delicate fragrance wafting through the air.

James was a conscientious, skilled gardener and the results were beautiful. The gardens were groomed to perfection. He was obviously pleased to share this lovely setting with a young, exuberant family.

Once they settled in, Maggie was taken outside each morning and seated in a comfortable chair beside the garden. At first, Sean and the children anxiously watched her, hoping to see her respond to the surrounding beauty. As one day flowed into the other, everyone started to accept her silent presence and few words. Sean still talked to her every night, telling her about the renovations he was overseeing at the mill, commenting on the weather, the crops and their family.

At times, she seemed to listen attentively, but the spark was gone from her eyes. She rarely looked at him directly. He saw the same lovely black hair, now threaded with silver, the prominent high cheekbones and the pale, unlined face that belied her 40 years of age. His Maggie was like a beautiful, hollow shell. Kissing her, when he arrived home from work and before he left each morning, he tried to imagine the woman she used to be, but that woman was simply not there.

One day a few weeks after their move, a letter arrived from Elizabeth. She was coming to visit them! Surprises, treats and special excursions were planned. Accompanied by Maeve and Frank, Sean picked her up at the train station while everyone else stayed home to help with the preparations.

Elizabeth's welcome was slightly overwhelming, but she was used to the ways of this large family. It felt wonderful to be in their presence again. She was toured through the house and around the gardens. They eagerly carried her bags to the bedroom that was prepared for her. After dinner, Alicia took her mother upstairs to prepare her for bed and Sean and Elizabeth went for a quiet walk. As they strolled arm in arm, Sean turned to her and spoke softly. "Maggie hasn't improved, has she? I keep watching and waiting, then days go by and I find myself accepting the way she is without a thought. That frightens me."

Elizabeth drew him over to a nearby bench. They sat down as she replied, "Sean, this is all so very sad. I miss her too, and have worried about her from a distance. That's one reason I came to visit. I've felt so lonely without each one of you. Needless to say, you're all in my prayers every night."

The following morning, Elizabeth lay in bed listening to the familiar 'cheer-up' sound of a robin outside her window. Its full, throaty whistle indicated there were probably three or four blue eggs in a nest nearby. In answer to the soft knock at her door, she called out, "Just a minute! I'm coming."

Slipping on a robe, she opened the door. There stood Maeve with a pitcher of hot water in her hands. Elizabeth opened the door wide and the girl entered, carefully setting the pitcher on the dresser beside the matching wash basin.

"Thank you, Maeve. How very thoughtful of you! Such a lovely gesture on my first morning here. I'm starving, and the delicious aromas wafting through the house are sheer torture! I'll wash up quickly, get dressed and meet you downstairs. Thanks again, dear."

Smiling at her, Maeve replied "See you in a while." She turned and left the room, closing the door gently behind her.

Elizabeth washed and dressed quickly. She brushed her long, blonde hair, then expertly twined and pinned the rolled tresses up into a shining knot at the back of her head. Her sky-blue dress matched the colour of her eyes. With a last glance in the mirror, she gently pinched her cheeks to add a little rosiness and left the room.

Sean had eaten earlier and was already at the mill. He usually left the house bright and early. Last night, he'd told Elizabeth that Maggie seldom ate her meals with the family. Alicia kept attempting to bring her down, without much success. He felt it was confusing for Maggie and a strain on everyone else. Usually, one of the older children took tea, some fruit and a biscuit or muffin to her room earlier in the morning. Sometimes she ate a bit of porridge, maybe a soft boiled egg, and nibbled on fruit or cheese, but her appetite was bird-like. They took turns sitting with her as she ate. That information concerned Elizabeth, but she needed time to think and plan. Possibly she'd find a way to ease and improve the situation.

Elizabeth was greeted with enthusiasm as she walked into the dining room. The buffet was laden with an assortment of foods, the picture of a real 'old country' breakfast. Everything looked and smelled appetizing. Sausages and kippers were flanked by a platter of scrambled eggs and a basket of homemade Irish tea biscuits. Several fresh fruits and a separate bowl of canned peaches sat beside strawberry jam and whipped butter. The tea was hot and full-bodied, served as Elizabeth remembered it. A pitcher of milk sat nearby. A tureen of hot oatmeal porridge was set beside bowls, accompanied by a pitcher of cream and a bowl of brown sugar. Her stomach growled as she viewed the food before her. They had prepared a very special, welcoming breakfast for her. Conversation was easy as the children took turns telling her about their new home.

After they were finished eating, Elizabeth helped with a few household chores, then returned upstairs to unpack. She paused, then tapped gently on the door to Maggie's room, waited a few seconds, then entered the room.

Her friend sat by the window gazing toward the gardens. She was dressed in a soft, moss green dress, her hair neatly braided, coiled and fastened behind each ear. It was a becoming style she'd often worn before. Apparently, the girls took turns helping her bathe, doing her hair and assisting her to dress.

Elizabeth's thoughts raced. 'What special children they are! Does Maggie see anything as she sits there staring outside? Is she actually recognizing any of the flowers? She used to enjoy gardening. How deep is this depression or sadness?' Tears filled her eyes as these thoughts flew helter-skelter through her mind. Taking a deep breath to calm herself, she knelt down beside Maggie's chair, gently reaching out to hold her hands. She recalled how these hands had so seldom been idle in the past.

They were cool to her touch, so she rubbed them with her own hands as she spoke. "Will you come out and walk with me, Maggie? Remember the grand hikes and walks we used to take together? We talked about everything. We are soulmates. Come and show me around. It's a beautiful day and Applewood seems like a lovely place." Leaning over and kissing her on the cheek, she continued speaking. "I've missed you."

Urging Maggie to stand, she held her hands and gently pulled her up. Half-expecting resistance, she was pleased with the response. Maggie stood and they walked downstairs, out the front door into the fresh air and warmth of the summer morning. Alicia waved at them from the clothesline, where she was hanging the washing to dry.

They strolled together through the gardens, toward the river.

"Soon you'll feel strong enough to walk to the mill."

They kept walking into a small copse of trees as Elizabeth continued the one-way conversation. "Look at the violets and the trilliums!" She talked on and on, praying there would be a response from the shell of a woman by her side. After a while, they simply walked arm and arm in silence. Perhaps this was enough.

Chapter
Seventeen

Elizabeth had known Frank for a few years, initially as his teacher in the one room schoolhouse, then as their friend. Early on, she recognized and admired his obvious artistic talent, but she'd thought of it as his hobby. Several days after Elizabeth's arrival, he took her up to his room and showed her his finished oil paintings, as well as several charcoal sketches. He then revealed a portfolio filled with pen and ink drawings. They were intricate, delicate and very beautiful.

As she looked through the collection of his work and studied each piece, she knew the young man's artistic skills reached way beyond the ordinary. He painted the world he lived in. His sketches seemed simple; however, with a few strokes, he could capture not only an accurate likeness, but also the emotions of his subjects. He was allowing her to view the works of an artist, a very talented artist.

There was a sketch of Alicia, sitting at the sewing machine deep in concentration, working on a blue velvet dress that looked so real, one could almost touch the softness. In another, Dorothy sat on a stool in the barn milking their cow, mischievously squirting milk at the row of cats as they sat waiting expectantly for a milky treat. The cobwebs in one small window glistened in the sunlight.

One picture in particular touched Elizabeth's heart. It was the figure of a man, standing with one hand on a fence, gazing into the distance. The utter dejection portrayed by his expression and his stance was gut-wrenching. It was Sean, pausing to rest, near the barn at their home in Quebec.

Oh Sean, she thought, continuing to study it for several moments, remembering those years.

She spoke as she turned toward Frank, "I'd like to arrange a showing for you. Your work should be shared, Frank, and it would afford you the opportunity to meet other artists. Will you allow me to do that?"

Frank looked at her incredulously, saying, "You really think they're good enough? A showing! Where?"

She smiled as she replied, "Yes, they are good enough. When you have twenty completed, that's enough for a decent display. You have more than that number right here. If I have my way, they'll be accepted. There are several studios here in Toronto whose curators encourage talented student artists."

Arriving home from work several days later, a pleasant scene met Sean's eyes. His children were all outside and Maggie was sitting with them. He kissed her cheek and for a brief moment, there was a flicker of recognition in her eyes. He quelled the thought, knowing better than to allow his hopes to rise. Suddenly she touched his cheek with her hand, softly saying, "Hello." Sean's heart soared.

Beth greeted him with a hug, saying, "Frank has a surprise for us, Dad! He's working on a special painting. He won't let any of us even peek at it."

Dorothy laughed, "He gets quite wicked when we try to sneak up on him!"

Frank glanced up from his easel. "Hi, Dad. I told Dotty that my painting won't mean anything to any of you until I've completely finished it. Another day or two, then I'll be ready to show it to you all."

Dorothy grinned at him. "Well hurry up and finish it Frank! We're all on pins and needles. Dad, pull up a chair and sit down. I'll pour you a cup of tea while it's still hot."

Sean moved a chair over beside Maggie and sat down, listening to the comforting sound of the voices around him. They made his life worth living. He sipped his tea and studied them one by one.

Frank continued painting. Everyone eagerly anticipated the unveiling of his most recent artistic venture. He'd been working on it for weeks. As Elizabeth moved closer to watch Frank's progress, Frank smiled and told her, "I'm actually going to unveil my painting tonight. It's finished. I want it to be a special surprise for everyone after dinner."

That evening, as they finished eating, Frank stood up, saying, "I'm going to show you my big canvas tonight. If I can excuse myself from the table, I will get everything ready. This is your invitation to come to the library as soon as the clean-up is done."

Dorothy spoke first, "Frank, that's wonderful! I can hardly wait. Hurry everybody, let's get everything cleared up!"

Frank laughed. "Don't rush in there too soon. It's not quite ready. First I have to carry my easel downstairs, then the painting, and then sign my name!"

As they gathered in the library, Elizabeth noticed that Frank had wisely placed the easel near the fireplace, where a lamp on the mantel cast light on the painting. When they were all seated, Frank proudly removed the sheet that covered his painting.

Sean gasped. There before him was a full length portrait of Maggie, seated on a chair in the garden. Every detail was perfect. The colour of her hair, the rings on her delicate fingers, the buttons on her dress, everything was perfect, except for her face. The face on the woman in the portrait was alive and vibrant. She had sparkling, blue eyes, so full of love, so expressive. Her mouth curved in a smile as she looked at them. Yes, this was Maggie, his Maggie. She was not the stone-faced woman who now stared at herself.

As usual, Dorothy was the first one to speak. "How did you do this, Frank? It's Mom before she got sick. I'd forgotten how she looked then. It's so beautiful. Maybe your painting will help her remember who she is and she'll come back to us. Oh, I love it. Thank you."

No one else could have expressed their thoughts more accurately. Frank had indeed brought their mother back to them. He accepted everyone's approval as they clustered around him.

Eventually, he sat down beside his father, while the girls left for the kitchen to prepare a bedtime treat in honour of the occasion.

"Dad, Elizabeth wants to organize a special show for my paintings. What is your opinion?"

Sean turned toward his son. "Well, Frank, I'm prejudiced because I am your father. Elizabeth has had more experience in judging such things. I imagine she has seen many budding artists in her day. If she says you should have a showing and helps to arrange it, I'll be the first one there. Every picture you draw or paint is like a miracle to me. This portrait of your mother is amazing." His voice broke as he spoke. "You have brought her back to us with your paintbrush and your love. We must work even more diligently to reach her and draw her back into our lives."

Sean returned to the library after everyone was in bed. Lighting the lamp, he gazed at the portrait of the woman he loved, and whispered, "Come back to us, Maggie. We all need you." Her eyes followed him as he left the room.

Elizabeth continued taking Maggie for daily walks. At least twice each week, she packed them a picnic. With the exercise and fresh air, Maggie's appetite slowly improved. There were times when she was so withdrawn, she refused to stroll even a short distance. Whenever that happened, Alicia or Maeve gave her a light lunch in her room and she rested there for the afternoon.

Chapter
Eighteen

A few weeks after their walks began, Elizabeth purposely prepared extra food. They ventured as far as the mill, just in case Sean cared to eat with them. It turned out to be a perfect idea. It was a light-hearted, carefree time and, from that day forward, he joined them regularly. Elizabeth often encouraged one or two of the girls to come along. These picnics were fast becoming the highlight of Sean's days. A weight seemed to lift from his shoulders as he relaxed. Elizabeth recognized that this busy man, the father of such a large family, needed these casual times. Maggie's husband was also her friend.

The lunch whistle blew as Sean washed his hands and face at the pump outside the mill. He headed off down the path to meet the picnickers partway. Passing a small, abandoned cottage along the way, he thought that it would be interesting to check it out, possibly make a few repairs, clean it up and show it to his daughters. Last night, Beth had told him that she was coming with Elizabeth and her mother today, so she was on his mind. He whistled as he strolled along.

Elizabeth's heart skipped a beat when she heard that happy sound! He'd been so quiet when she first arrived to visit. Life and sorrow were taking a toll on him.

Smiling, he greeted her, "Hello Elizabeth. Where's Beth?"

"Alicia planned an apple picking excursion, picnic and all. Beth couldn't make up her mind what to do, but she finally decided to go with the others because Maggie is resting and didn't feel like a walk with us today."

"I'm glad you came anyway. Thanks for that, but you'll miss picking apples with them."

Elizabeth laughed. "I adore those children of yours, Sean, but I admit it's good to get away from them all, once in a while!"

A crash of thunder made them both jump. The sky had looked a bit threatening off to the west, but suddenly the storm was close.

"Come on," yelled Sean. "There's an abandoned cottage back there a bit. Let's run for it!"

Taking the picnic basket from her, he grasped her hand and they raced toward the building, just as the skies broke loose and the rain poured down. They arrived breathless and laughing. Finding the door ajar, Sean pushed it open and they stepped inside. The room was empty, except for one rickety table that leaned against a side wall.

Sean shouted above the sound of the storm outside, "Welcome to The Old Mill Cafe!"

Elizabeth shook the water from her dress and hair. "Look, Sean, there's a fireplace."

A pile of wood and a basket of twigs stood on the floor beside it. Sean carefully arranged the dry twigs and a few logs. Searching his pockets, he found some matches and soon the cheery flames took the dampness away. The rain continued to drum on the roof. Sean was surprised that the sturdy little cabin had a roof that didn't leak.

Elizabeth spread a quilt on the floor. They sat down and talked comfortably about many subjects as they ate their delicious lunch of egg salad sandwiches, pickles, cheese, fruit and butter tarts. When the last morsel was eaten, they realized the rain had lessened.

Sean mentioned that he hadn't heard the 'end of lunch break' mill whistle. Then he added, "The workers will probably leave for home, as it's too wet to continue their outside renovations." Standing up, he stretched, then reached down, grasping Elizabeth's hands and pulling her to her feet.

Suddenly they were holding each other tight. He kissed her lips and felt her sweet response. His hand pulled the pins from her hair and it fell in damp waves down her back. He buried his face in its fragrance. They looked into each other's eyes, hesitated for a moment, simply holding one another, then they sank back to the floor. In silent agreement, they touched and kissed, explored and felt, slowly removing their clothes. Sean touched Elizabeth gently, sensing this was a new experience for her. They responded to a need that neither one attempted to comprehend. Holding his own urgent desire in check, he slowly taught her how to make love until she shuddered and called out his name.

When the rain stopped and the storm passed, Sean held a silently weeping Elizabeth in his arms. "What kind of a friend am I?" she whispered.

"Hush, dear one. We mustn't feel ashamed. Please don't regret this precious time. I've never been unfaithful to Maggie before. Sometimes, lately, I feel like I'm mourning her as if she were dead. God forgive me, but it's true! Can you understand such feelings? I promise this won't happen again, if those are your wishes." His voice was shaky as he continued, "Thank you for giving yourself to me, Elizabeth. These have been difficult years for us all. I'm not making excuses. You have brought me comfort."

She nodded her head without speaking. Slowly running her hand through his hair and down his face, she pulled him toward her and kissed his lips. They held each other for a few more moments before she stood up, stepped back and began to dress.

He stood nearby, watching her, then began putting his own clothes back on. As she braided her hair, he helped her retrieve the pins and combs from the floor. She straightened his collar, then turned around so he could fasten the long row of buttons that secured the back of her dress. Each gesture was treasured.

The wood was burnt down to ashes. A small wooden fragment or two remained. The occasional snap and crackle sounded loud in the room. Elizabeth turned to face Sean again. Blue eyes met grey. He simply enfolded her in his arms and held her close once more. When they slipped outside, it was raining steadily again.

They walked hand in hand to the fork in the road. He turned toward the mill and she walked away on the homeward path. After several steps, they spontaneously turned and looked back toward one another as they waved goodbye.

Elizabeth arrived home drenched to the skin. She mounted the stairs quickly, entered her room and softly closed the door. Stepping over to the mirror, she touched her flushed cheeks. Smiling to herself, she remembered the afternoon, the picnic and the rain. She latched the door, stepped out of her soaking wet dress and peeled off her undergarments. She washed herself in the cold water that was left in the pitcher. Each motion of the washcloth gave her a new awareness of her body, of herself. Wherever she touched, she thought of Sean and felt his hands on her. She pulled on a nightgown, lay on the bed, drew the quilt over herself and fell sound asleep.

Elizabeth wakened to the sound of voices. The girls and Frank were home! She dressed quickly, arriving downstairs eager to hear about their adventures. Dinner was a festive affair. The children's stories were delightful, full of anecdotes about their day. They had also been caught in the rain. Fortunately, they were near the doctor's house when the downpour began. They quickly sought shelter there, and although Dr. Mack was not home, his housekeeper welcomed them inside.

Mrs. Wilson was delighted to see them and was soon bustling around, as she insisted on preparing a treat. Hot tea, a pitcher of milk and a large plate of fresh oatmeal cookies were set before them. A nearby jar held date filling which was meant to be spread on top of one cookie or between two cookies.

"These are the Doc's favourite," she said, with a broad smile.

Dr. Mack had arrived home as they were finishing their tea. He was pleased to see the visitors, coaxing them to stay a bit longer. Soon, he was telling them some real life stories about his day to day experiences.

He asked about Maggie and Alicia explained, "Mother is home resting, and Cathy is there with her, seeing to her needs."

When speaking with Sean previously, Dr. Mack had suggested that Sean hire a neighbourhood girl to come to their house several days each week. The older children shared so many responsibilities, he believed this young woman would ease the added stress they'd all been dealing with for quite a while. She could help care for Maggie and do extra jobs around the house.

Today's outing had obviously lifted everyone's spirits. Sean suggested that after the dishes were done, they should all join him in the library.

Prior to gathering with the others, Elizabeth followed her routine, helping Maggie prepare for bed. She chatted as she brushed her friend's hair, braided it loosely and tucked her into bed. Maggie's lack of response was the same as usual.

Returning downstairs, Elizabeth followed the sound of Sean's voice reading aloud from 'Oliver Twist.' The snap and crackle of the fire, the sound of the rain pelting the windows and the deep resonance of his voice, all added to the comforting ambience. When it was time for bed, a sleepy, satisfied group headed upstairs.

As she lay in bed, Elizabeth decided to visit Dr. Mack in the morning. Something more defined must be done for Maggie. There was no sense in fooling themselves any longer. Her ailment was not simply a passing depression.

She closed her eyes and allowed her mind to drift back to the hours she and Sean had spent together that afternoon.

In another room of the house, Sean slept peacefully for the first time in months. All in all, it had been a very memorable day.

Chapter
Nineteen

The following morning, Elizabeth walked the two miles to Dr. Mack's house. He had become a good friend and she hoped to seek his advice. It was a beautiful, clear summer day. She heard the calls of the birds as they flocked together in the trees. Reaching the doctor's house, she was greeted at the door by his housekeeper.

"Good morning, Miss Elizabeth."

"Good morning, Mrs. Wilson. Would it be possible for me to speak with Dr. Mack, if he's in?"

"Of course. He hasn't left on his morning rounds yet. Please come into the study and have a seat. I'll tell him you're here."

Several minutes later, she heard voices and a door opening and closing. As Dr. Mack entered the study, he noticed her strained smile and the concern in her eyes.

Taking her hands in his, he said, "This is a visit I've been hoping for, Elizabeth. I was about to have a cup of tea. Will you join me?"

Without waiting for an answer, he turned to Mrs. Wilson, who hovered by the door. "Tea and some of your delightful scones would please us no end, Mrs. Wilson." With a twinkle in her eye, she hurried from the room.

Dr. Mack looked at Elizabeth. "Is there trouble in that active household?"

She took a deep breath before replying. "No more than usual, Dr. Mack, but something more has to be done for Maggie. She's been like this, on and off, for too long! I don't think she's improved at all since I last saw her in Quebec. It isn't fair to her, to Sean, or their children."

She continued speaking, telling him about the rare moments when Maggie seemed to be listening, or the times when her eyes focused, as if actually recognizing one of them. She recalled specific, frightening incidents when Maggie displayed sudden, rare moments of anger and frustration by throwing a hairbrush across the room or turning a plateful of food upside down and refusing to eat.

He listened intently, nodding his head once in a while. Elizabeth stopped speaking as unwanted tears spilled from her eyes and rolled down her cheeks. "It's so difficult for everyone."

Dr. Mack methodically knocked the ashes from his pipe into a dish on his desk then packed it with fresh tobacco.

"Do you mind if I smoke?" As she shook her head, he lit the pipe and took a few puffs before he spoke. "Sean refuses to have her institutionalized. I've tried to convince him to do this as a last resort, but he's a very stubborn man. And proud. Perhaps it's the pride that stands in his way, even more than the stubborn streak. He can't or won't admit that perhaps someone else might draw her out when he is unable to reach her. If he took this step and allowed her to go to the place I've suggested, she might have a chance."

Elizabeth wiped her eyes and blew her nose before replying, "I know she can hear us. Most of the time she lives in a trance, eating, moving, walking like a mechanical doll. I can't help thinking that if she can do these few things, why can't she accomplish more? Sometimes I feel like shaking her. I know she can talk because I've heard her, though she never really speaks to anyone directly. Most of the time she is silent, but sometimes she mumbles and whispers. When I hear her, I wonder if she's purposely shutting everyone out. It is difficult enough for me. She's my friend. I can only imagine what it's like, day in and day out, for Sean and the children."

Mrs. Wilson arrived with the tea tray. Dr. Mack thanked her, then poured them each a cup of steaming tea. "Elizabeth, I sincerely wish

I could answer your questions. An illness like the one Maggie is suffering from, and I do believe it is an illness, is considered by many professionals to be a genetic weakness. With some patients, this is possibly true, but in her case I beg to differ. Maggie's situation was brought on by trauma. I have no definite facts to base my ideas on, but a family doctor, particularly a country doctor like me, sees many patients, as well as a vast number and variety of interesting cases. Innumerable traumatic events have bombarded that whole family, not just Maggie."

He reached into a desk drawer and drew out a piece of paper. "I was thinking about Maggie a week or two ago after Sean and I spent some time together one evening. We were relaxed with one another and discussed a variety of subjects. Eventually, he mentioned Maggie and we talked about her situation. His pain is very evident. I listened carefully, hearing about the heartbreaks he and the family suffered and are still suffering. When I came home, I was restless and unable to sleep, so I jotted down my observations: being separated, the number of children, the responsibilities, Sean's illness, Maeve's illness, the death of baby Muriel, and finally Maggie's brother and his family, dying such a horrible death only a few months ago. She was still in the throes of mourning when they moved here. As you can see, it's quite a long list!"

He sat quietly puffing on his pipe for a few minutes, letting his words sink in, then continued on, "You are a blessing for them all, Elizabeth. I know that's why you packed up and came here. You're determined to help."

He stood up and began pacing up and down the room. "People are suddenly stricken by something like this and often it's labelled a nervous breakdown. Some never recover, while others, with similar signs, heal and become as good as new. You can understand that the medical community has a great deal to learn about these so-called nervous disorders. Well, I am frustrated. It has been a lot for all of them to cope with. Now, Maggie, the one who kept the household going throughout each change and challenge, finally slipped down under and she hasn't been able to make it back up to the surface."

He replaced the paper in his file. "I need your help, Elizabeth. I believe if we can convince Sean to at least visit the facility I recommended, he might consider taking her there. There's a possibility that this place is perfect for Maggie. I know you are very close with the family and they appreciate your involvement with Maggie. Perhaps Sean will listen to you. Will you help me?"

Elizabeth leaned over, placing her hand on his arm. "Dr. Mack, if you believe the doctors at this care centre can help Maggie, I will do my best to convince Sean to at least visit it."

He smiled and offered her a ride home in his carriage, mentioning that if she didn't mind, he had one stop to make before reaching her destination.

As they rode along, Dr. Mack brought the subject up again. "If Sean agrees, I will accompany you both on the first trip there. It's truly a 'house of healing.' Originally, it was opened by a doctor and his wife to care for expectant mothers. The women are encouraged to arrive when labour is in the very early stages. A skilled midwife guides each one through the birthing process. After the baby is born, mother and baby stay there for approximately two weeks. It is a special bonding time for them as they quietly get to know each other again, in a different way. I use the term 'again' because I believe that a mother and her child already know one another from those inseparable nine months prior to birth. There are those who scoff at such a thought, but in time, we'll learn more about this. How can that unborn child not know this unique person, who carries him or her inside her body, as they go through this miracle together? Whether it's a first baby or a fifth one, this break from the regular routine at home helps the mother gain her strength, mind, body and soul. Each woman is encouraged to eat properly, exercise, and accept guidance from the personal assistants, the doctor and the midwives. The Meadows has been up and running for seven years now and has sixteen rooms. Two years ago, six of those rooms were set aside to care for women with emotional disorders. Some of them are women who returned home to their family life after giving birth, but for one reason or another suffered a type of breakdown. In desperation, their family doctor was called, and a few have referred these women to that resting, healing home."

He thought for a moment or two, then continued, "The owners are fine people. He's a doctor and his wife is a midwife and a registered nurse. In their line of work, they recognize the importance of a mother's care for herself and her baby, before and after birth. When they decided to deal with the other issues, they hired another doctor, a specialist with a specific interest in depression and other related mental illnesses. In this newest section of the facility, each patient stays for an unpredictable length of time. They recognize the importance of privacy so these rooms are located in a separate section of the house. They know me now, as I initially checked the place over, and have since recommended it for several of my expectant mothers. If Sean agrees, Maggie will be my first patient to try this relatively new area."

They rode along in silence for a while. Dr. Mack had given Elizabeth both food for thought as well as hope.

Chapter
Twenty

They sat quietly side by side, enjoying the peaceful scene that unfolded around them as they travelled along the country lane. The horse seemed to know exactly where they were going.

When Elizabeth commented on this, Dr. Mack chuckled. "You are so right! Of course, sometimes there are emergencies, but Beauty here can tell the difference. If I don't rush her, she senses we are making regular calls. I suppose she knows me really well. Usually, when we head this direction, the first stop is the Bakers' house. Wait and see what she does when we arrive there. Anyway, I think you will find this couple to be quite interesting."

Sure enough, the horse slowed and turned into the next lane, with no obvious guidance from Dr. Mack. The lane was overgrown with weeds, but Beauty plodded on toward the house. Here and there, Elizabeth caught glimpses of cats. As more appeared, she noted the various sizes and colours. When they arrived at the tired-looking house, Beauty stopped by an old hitching post.

The doctor stepped down from the driver's side and moved around the carriage to help Elizabeth. The house was obviously in dire need of repairs, as some faded blue shutters looked to be holding on by a sliver while several others were lying on the ground below. As they picked their way up the remains of a walkway, she viewed the remnants of an overgrown garden on each side. Here and there, amidst the weeds, a lovely flower bravely lifted its full-blown beauty above the chaos that surrounded it.

The fragile porch was decorated with many cats who curiously stopped their playing, grooming, and eating to silently observe the visitors. Several kittens scurried away to hide, while two of the older cats, obviously recognizing Dr. Mack, strolled over to rub against his legs.

The front door squeaked open as they were greeted by an older gentleman. "Come in, come in, sir. I see you've brought a young lady, a guest. Well now, isn't this a pleasant surprise."

He turned his head and called out, "Look, dear, I believe one of your fans is here to see you. The good doctor has arrived with a lady." As he spoke, he led them through a tiny hall into the parlour, where a very old lady sat by the window in a rocking chair. Two cats were cuddled on her lap, while several kittens played or slept at her feet. Stepping carefully to avoid the cats, Elizabeth followed their host into the cluttered room. Never had she seen so many feline creatures, all in the same place. She was flabbergasted! With a swift, but gentle swoop of his arm, Mr. Baker cleared two chairs of cats and motioned for the guests to sit down. He offered to make tea, but Dr. Mack declined both the chair and the tea, explaining that he had several other house calls to make. He was there to check on Mrs. Baker.

As the doctor proceeded to attend to the woman, her husband handed a scrapbook to Elizabeth. Opening the yellowed, tattered book to a specific page, he pointed a gnarled finger at a photograph. "See this picture? That's my Daisy, singing at her first concert in New York City. Stay a moment while I play one of her songs."

He walked over to an ancient Victrola, wound it up and carefully placed the needle on a record. The room was suddenly alive with the sound of a glorious soprano voice. The record was old and scratchy, but the essence of the music brought unexpected tears to Elizabeth's eyes. She leafed carefully through the book as her ears filled with the aria from a well-known opera.

Suddenly, the needle stuck in a crack and Mrs. Baker stopped stroking the cats, lifted her head and waited, motionless. Even the cats seemed to stop moving until the old gentleman corrected the situation and the music continued. Once more, Mrs. Baker relaxed and began stroking her pets. The kittens returned to chasing dusty rainbows as the sun streamed through a window.

They left the house with promises to return for tea someday, walking in silence to the carriage. Once they were both seated and Beauty was headed back toward the main road, Elizabeth turned toward Dr. Mack. "I feel as if I'm dreaming. Did I really see and hear what I think I did?"

Dr. Mack grinned at her, nodding his head. "You certainly did. They arrived here about ten years ago. I had recently graduated from medical school and moved here myself to begin my practice. There was a flurry of excitement in our little community when rumours spread with the news that an American opera singer was retiring here. Apparently, several years earlier, after one of her guest appearances in Toronto, Mr. Baker had brought his wife to this area for a much needed rest. They stayed at the old inn a few miles away and were treated very well. This beautiful, peaceful place was a far cry from the busy life they led, travelling all over the world as she performed. She literally fell in love with this part of the world. After Daisy retired due to age and failing health, her husband decided to bring her back to this area."

They rode in silence, then Dr. Mack continued his story. "That little house was a picture in those days. The people around here had high hopes that she'd perhaps join one of the churches and put on a few concerts. That never happened. They'd come here to get away from everything. He told a few folks at the store that his wife was tired and elderly, like himself. She had the good sense to realize that her voice, like her body, was wearing down. The community respected their wishes for privacy. It was still exciting for them to know she had chosen to live here. Occasionally, they glimpsed her from afar when the couple took a buggy ride. Mr. Baker always made the trips to town by himself. We knew he was being very protective of her."

He paused for a few moments, then continued speaking, "Anyway, about two years after their arrival, Mr. Baker came rushing over to my house. He was so upset he could barely speak. I thought he was going to have a heart attack, so I left him with my house-keeper, suggesting that he should sit quietly and have a cup of tea before returning home, and I'd go ahead to their house. He didn't argue. I hastened there and found Daisy lying on the bedroom floor. Upon examination, I determined she'd had a stroke. With time, she gained some basic use of her arms and legs, but she was unable to walk alone or feed herself. She has never spoken a word since then. I visit each week. Once, I suggested that they should hire extra help to keep the place up and care for them. He refused. A couple of weeks ago, I asked him how many cats they have. He replied that, at last count, they had sixty-two! As you probably noticed, he's made little hinged doors so the animals can go in and out, as they please. It's the strangest thing, Elizabeth, some of those cats never enter the house, or eat the food he sets out. They are the hunters. He calls them 'the mousers.' You have now been introduced to one of our neighbour-hood celebrities."

Prior to leaving that morning, Elizabeth had written a note for the family, informing them that she was off to visit Dr. Mack for morning tea. When they arrived back at Applewood, she thanked the doctor and went inside. He continued on his way to make a few more calls.

Meanwhile, during the morning, Alicia had prepared a picnic lunch for Beth, Elizabeth, Maggie, Dorothy and Sean. Maggie was not always able to go on their picnics, but that day, she seemed ready to accompany them.

Kathleen had some music to practice, Frank was painting and Alicia had sewing to finish, so they were eager to spend some time on their own. They also planned to make a few preparations toward the evening meal.

Beth ran ahead and Dorothy carried the picnic basket while Elizabeth and Maggie walked along with their arms entwined.

Sean greeted each of them with a hug when they arrived at the mill. "You beautiful ladies are a welcome sight. It's a hungry man I am today. We've had a busy morning."

Dorothy laughed. "By the weight of this basket, Alicia has packed enough for at least three starving men, so we should have plenty!"

Her father took the basket from her and they soon chose the perfect spot in the shade for a sunny day's picnic. The food tasted especially good. As so often happens, when people enjoy nature and each other's company, speech was not necessary. Even the quiet moments were special. Maggie seemed to relax and eat more in these surroundings.

They were finished when the mill's 'end of lunch' whistle echoed through the woods. Sean helped Maggie to her feet and gently hugged her. Dorothy took her mother's arm and began the return walk home, with Beth beside them.

As Elizabeth finished tidying, Sean took the basket from her and set it on the ground. This was the moment she'd been dreading, yet waiting for. Yesterday seemed far away, a special dream that had arrived, then flitted away, never to be forgotten. Sean hugged her briefly as their eyes met.

Her carefully planned explanations were forgotten as she blurted out, "I love you, Sean. You know that. I also care deeply for your family. Please allow me this one favour. Forgive me for interfering, but I hardly slept last night, thinking of Maggie. I went to see Dr. Mack this morning, planning to ask for advice about exactly how we can help her. Something more has to be done. You know that too. This whole situation is difficult for everyone. Please, please, let's try something different. Will you arrange for Dr. Mack to take us both to see The Meadows rest home? He believes this might give her a chance at recovery." Her lovely blue eyes glistened with tears as she reached out and held his hand.

Sean's voice was barely a whisper as he replied, "You and I both miss the Maggie we used to know. If it weren't for the children and you, Elizabeth..." He couldn't finish speaking, but in a few moments, he raised his eyes to hers, cleared his throat, and then spoke with conviction. "Please help us. Do whatever you can. Heaven knows I'm at a loss. Ask Mack to arrange an appointment. I realize you love her too. I love you both."

He longed to take her in his arms, but the moment slipped away as Dorothy called out from down the path, "Bye, Dad. See you later. Are you coming, Elizabeth?"

They squeezed hands and left each other with a new song in their hearts.

Chapter
Twenty-One

Dr. Mack was pleased to receive a note from Elizabeth the following morning. She thanked him for the hospitality and the interesting ride home, adding that she and Sean would both be free to visit The Meadows as soon as he could make arrangements.

Two days later, he arrived at the house, driving his Ford car to pick up Elizabeth and Sean. They drove off, ready to face the day and its impending decisions together. The large, stately, old building stood a fair distance back from the main road, on property that was neatly enclosed by an imposing stone wall. They drove up to a small building that was tended by a gatekeeper.

He checked the doctor's identification, acknowledging him with a smile, then swung the gate wide open. The doctor thanked him, then addressed Elizabeth and Sean, saying, "That's a safety procedure for the privacy of the women who stay here. It also keeps anyone from wandering off. Apparently, this was quite a popular inn years ago and many fine parties were held here. The Prime Minister and his wife were known to bring other dignitaries for dinners and special occasions."

He parked the vehicle in a specific area, well away from the house and any horse-drawn carriages that might arrive. Leading Elizabeth up the steps to the huge front doors, Dr. Mack used the bell to announce their arrival. A pleasant woman greeted them, took their wraps, and then led the way down the hall to an office. The owners, Dr. Penfold and his wife, Mary, both stood as introductions were made. A brief conversation revealed their enthusiasm and dedication to this special home and the programs it offered.

Their tour was reassuring. They were first guided through the bright and cheery maternity section. The bedrooms were not large, but ample for sleeping and resting, as each held a bed, two easy chairs, a dresser and a desk. Windows in each room revealed a peaceful, countryside scene. Common rooms were comfortably furnished with leather couches and easy chairs. A piano in each common room added to a homey ambience. Bouquets of flowers sat on the hall table, in the sitting rooms and in the dining room. They were shown the nursery, where the babies were kept and tended to while their mothers rested or took part in other activities.

Then they were led through a set of locked, double doors that opened to the area reserved for the residents who stayed for longer periods of time. This section was similar to the one they'd just walked through, with accommodations for a maximum of six patients. The facility was spotlessly clean.

When the tour ended, they were led to a library that opened off the main office where they discussed Maggie's condition. When their talk concluded, Sean agreed to give it a try. Papers were signed and a date was set for Maggie's arrival.

As they left the building, the sound of music followed them out the front door. Someone was playing the piano. Sean felt this was a good omen. Elizabeth's heartache eased slightly as she pictured Maggie in such a healing environment.

Maggie settled into The Meadows easily, without any fuss. They were not allowed to visit her for three weeks. Dr. Mack promised to check on her once or twice, not to visit, but to speak with the doctor and to hear a progress report.

After his initial visit during the second week, he dropped in that evening to speak with Elizabeth and Sean. He was greeted warmly and ushered into the library. Sean poured a brandy for himself and Mack, and a sherry for Elizabeth. Dr. Mack's news was reassuring. Maggie had said 'thank you' and 'please' to one of the housemaids.

Not once, but several times. He cautioned them not to get their hopes up too high, then added that the doctors were optimistic.

Sean was serious as he asked, "Why do you think she's responding there and not here?"

Expecting to hear that question, Dr. Mack replied, "I believe there's nothing there to frighten her. There are no chores she should be working at, no children looking at her with pleading eyes, no loving husband or dear friend watching her every move. Nothing is expected of her and everything is different. It is a new life and a different lifestyle. I realize that sounds callous, but it isn't, really. I asked the same question while I was there and that's exactly what I was told by Dr. Penfold's wife. She has been reading aloud to Maggie and spending quite a bit of time with her. She informed me that, a few days ago, when one of the helpers arrived to prepare Maggie for breakfast, she was up, washed, dressed and attempting to do her own hair. She has continued doing that each morning since. I also learned that, as well as being a nurse, midwife and Dr. Penfold's wife, Dr. Betty studied psychology several years ago, receiving her doctorate in that field. Maggie is in good hands."

His answer eased their anxieties.

The end of July arrived and, finally, the initial three weeks were up and family members were allowed to visit. They were all eager to see their mother, but Dr. Mack decided that, for this initial family visitation, they should keep the numbers down. He promised that, as more frequent visits came about, he'd pick some of them up in his car and they'd go to see their mom. The thoughts of riding in a car for the first time placated everybody.

Filled with anticipation, anxiety and excitement, Alicia, Elizabeth and Sean rode through the warmth of the summer's day with Dr. Mack. The air blew through the open windows of the car, keeping them comfortable as they travelled toward their destination.

Entering the front hall of the building, Dr. Mack explained the layout to Alicia. She was thrilled to catch glimpses of several of the mothers with their newborn babies, walking them outside, or rocking them in their arms. A momentary pang of sadness flowed through her as she thought of the wee sister she had never seen.

Her heart was racing when the doctor opened the door to the area Maggie lived in. She listened quietly as Dr. Mack told her a few success stories of women who had healed and were back home with their loved ones.

The sound of piano music reached their ears as they were greeted by one of the assistants. She took them to the office where Dr. Penfold and Dr. Betty awaited them. They stood, speaking their greetings and shaking hands with each one, as Dr. Mack introduced Alicia to them. Instead of asking them to sit down, Dr. Betty simply said, "Follow me, please."

They proceeded to do so, walking down the hall and entering the sitting room. Three women sat near the piano, listening to the music. Maggie was not one of them. She was the pianist!

The doctor guided them to an area furnished with a couch and chairs. After they were settled, as the music continued, she quietly said to them, "Maggie has been dressing herself, as you know. Earlier this week, one of the aides took her outside for a daily outing. When they returned, a few of the ladies were having afternoon tea together in this room. The aide decided to casually take Maggie into the room and seat her with them. As they walked by the piano, Maggie stopped, turned, sat down on the piano stool and began playing. It was a special moment. She has been encouraged to come here every day since. Without hesitation, she always heads for the piano and gifts everyone with at least fifteen minutes of music. This is an unexpected and wonderful breakthrough."

When Maggie finished playing, instead of bringing her to see them, the aide led her out of the room. It was almost time for lunch and a regular schedule was important for Maggie's well-being. Dr. Penfold invited them to stay for a private lunch. They would have a short visit with Maggie immediately following the meal.

True to his word, they were taken to a cozy sitting room after their tasty lunch. Maggie sat in a rocker. She looked up as they approached her. Alicia bent down and kissed her mother's cheek. Maggie reached for her hand and held it for a moment, then Elizabeth stepped over and hugged her. After a few moments, Sean leaned over, giving her a gentle kiss.

She spoke clearly. "Hello, Sean." Her right hand reached up and touched his cheek. It was enough for everyone. They sat for a short while, taking turns telling her about home. She didn't say much, but she listened. After about ten minutes, the aide arrived to take her away for an afternoon rest. The three of them stood watching as they left the room. Then Maggie hesitated, turned around and, lifting one hand, waved to them.

The return home was a joyous one. Sean thanked Elizabeth and Mack for encouraging him to finally seek professional help for Maggie. They eagerly shared their good news with the rest of the family at dinner that evening.

Chapter
Twenty-Two

Elizabeth planned to return to Quebec soon to settle a few personal affairs. Prior to coming to Ontario, she had notified the School Board that she would no longer be teaching in the one-room schoolhouse. Upon their request, she willingly agreed to return and assist the incoming teacher for the month of September. It was a different experience being the only teacher responsible for students in all those grades, especially when they were in the same room! A newcomer could possibly feel quite alone, without being surrounded by fellow teachers. The challenge had been quite disconcerting for Elizabeth for the first few weeks, but she had planned well and adapted quickly. Because of her own positive experience, she was willing to assist the teacher who was hired to fill her shoes.

Word travelled quickly. Several parents in the Applewood area asked her to consider tutoring their children when she returned in October. It seemed like a logical thing to do and she was definitely considering their requests. She hoped and prayed that Maggie would be almost herself by then. Deep within, she contemplated the fact that her friend's health was possibly an ongoing, lifelong healing process.

Dr. Mack felt comfortable with their lively family and he called on them often. He and Sean were becoming good friends. They fished together occasionally, arriving home with the welcome catch of rainbow trout, fresh from the nearby fast-flowing stream.

Before Elizabeth left for Quebec, he made ongoing plans with her. They enjoyed drives in the country, going out for dinner, or eating at his home where Mrs. Wilson's delicious meals awaited them. Spending time together was easy and natural.

One evening, as they sat in the library together after playing a game of chess, Elizabeth stood, saying it was time for her to leave.

Mack helped her on with her cape, then took her in his arms and held her close. The familiar scent of tobacco and the strength of his arms were comforting. He kissed her, then said, "I believe I fell in love with you on our buggy ride, that first day we spent time together alone. I love you, Elizabeth. Perhaps this isn't the proper way to propose to you, but I'm doing it anyway. We're comfortable together and I've learned to love and respect you more and more as the weeks go by. Don't give me an answer right now, but think about it. I believe it's time we both settled down—with each other! Will you consider marrying me?"

Elizabeth stood back, feeling respect and love for this man.

"Dr. Mack, oh dear, I'll probably never call you anything but that. I feel honoured that you've asked me to marry you. There's no need to talk about it later. I'm flustered because I've never been proposed to before!"

She reached out and touched his hands. "You have wonderful, strong hands. Gentle yet strong. I've watched these hands cool a fevered forehead, grasp a shoulder, or administer to an injured body. Each time you hold my hand or put your arms around me, I feel secure and protected. I love you too. I accept your proposal with all my heart."

They settled their future with another kiss.

The following evening, Elizabeth sat on the verandah as night fell softly. Sean came out the door carrying a small snifter of brandy for each of them. They sat quietly, watching fireflies dancing through the air, their little lights giving a magical touch to the fairy-like wonder of the evening. A sense of peace and well-being warmed their hearts.

Sean teased her. "I think Mack is courting you. What do you say about that?"

Elizabeth sipped the brandy, allowing the heat to calm her thoughts. "I think so too, Sean. It's time for us to talk. About everything. I'm not certain what to say or how to begin."

Neither of them had ever mentioned their afternoon in the rain, yet miraculously, there was no strain between them. The summer's activities had focused on Maggie's health.

Sean was the first to speak. "Mack has become my dear friend. He has shared the fact that he has fallen in love with you. There was no need for him to tell me, as I've watched the two of you together. Elizabeth, I will be very thankful if you two decide to share your lives." He stopped speaking for a few moments, letting his words sink into both of their minds. "What happened between us is ours to cherish. I refuse to call that afternoon a weak moment. It was much more than that and I will never forget it. Let's not ruin it with either worries or regrets. Thank you for those precious moments we shared. What we experienced was a gift, a respite from the sadness and storms we were both experiencing. We both loved Maggie then and we love her now. You, as her dearest friend. Me, as her husband. She needs us more than ever now."

Sean raised his glass, touched it to hers and toasted, "To you and Mack." The subject was closed. Elizabeth knew she could move on with her new life. They walked inside, leaving the fireflies dancing in the night.

Chapter
Twenty-Three

Elizabeth and Dr. Mack made their wedding plans. 'Christmas at Applewood' seemed to be the perfect time for a small wedding celebration. She left the last weekend in August to spend the pre-arranged month in the one-room schoolhouse in Quebec. By this time, Maggie had improved enough to come home from The Meadows for several two-day visits. Everything went well; however, Dr. Betty recommended that Maggie should return to the nursing facility until the holidays, as she was still very fragile. Everyone hoped that, by Christmas, she'd be able to stay home for a week.

Mack wrote letters to Elizabeth telling her of his daily activities, visits to see Maggie, the books he was reading, anecdotes about Sean's family, and a few comments about his patients. He often mentioned how eagerly he anticipated their wedding on Christmas Eve.

Elizabeth's letters revealed that an older man was the new teacher. Wisdom, intelligence and a good sense of humour were attributes that assured his acceptance. He was obviously well-liked by the students.

The Christmas season was a happy one as old routines and celebrations continued. The children willingly pulled together to prepare the food and decorate the house. Everyone eagerly anticipated the wedding of their two dear friends.

It was wonderful to have Elizabeth and Maggie both arrive home a few days before Christmas. Maggie rested for a while each afternoon, but she joined them for the evening meals. She even played the piano for a couple of their family sing-songs. The house rang with laughter, music and a new sense of well-being.

The wedding ceremony for Elizabeth and Dr. Mack was held in the parlour at two in the afternoon. The only guests were the family members, James, Mrs. Wilson and her husband, Will, and Cathy, the young woman who had been assisting with Maggie and the household duties.

Kathleen played the piano as the glowing bride walked down the staircase and into the parlour on James's arm. Their two attendants, Maggie and Sean, stood waiting for them by the small wooden archway at the far end of the room. Sean and Frank had built the archway and the girls had woven fresh green holly branches, bursting with red berries, throughout the latticework design.

Elizabeth was lovely in her elegant, white lace gown. Maggie wore a sapphire blue velvet dress. Both gowns had been designed and made by Alicia. The three men wore dark suits with crisp white shirts and plaid ties for each one, red for Dr. Mack, blue for Sean and green for James. The solemn vows were exchanged, then the minister from the local church pronounced them man and wife. A small reception was held, during which toasts were made, food was eaten and songs were sung. The bride and groom slipped away for the night, promising to return for dinner on Christmas Day. They'd postponed their honeymoon until the summer, with plans to go north for a couple of weeks at that time.

Maggie was quite content to return to The Meadows after the wedding. She continued receiving treatment and care there until the end of April. Dr. Betty and Dr. Penfold assured both Sean and Maggie that, even after she returned home to stay, she was welcome to return for respite care. In fact, they advised Dr. Mack that this practice was not only wise, but necessary.

Chapter
Twenty-Four

Sean followed the world events with a watchful eye, as the newspapers were full of threatening news. The Germans had increased the size of their navy over the past few years. The Russo-Japanese War had weakened Russia and increased Germany's power in relation to other European countries. England, France and Russia had become friends. With such close proximity to France, England knew that any threat toward France also endangered England. When Austria declared war on Serbia, Russia began to mobilize forces. This led to a similar mobilization of forces in Germany. On August 1, Germany declared war against Russia and then, on August 3, they declared war against France. England sought a conference with the leaders of the powers involved. France agreed to a meeting, but Germany refused. With all these events occurring so rapidly, it was not a surprise when England declared war against Germany on August 4, 1914. Canadians heard the news with both sadness and a sense of pride.

It was not long before this war across the ocean affected Canada, putting fear into the hearts of all. Industry improved quickly, as factories produced ammunition, clothing, guns, food, tents, camping gear and all the other articles necessary for the daily existence of soldiers. Thirty thousand volunteers sailed from Canada's shores to form the Canadian Expeditionary Force. The drums of war heightened awareness with mixed feelings of courage and fear, as well as a sense of excitement and adventure. Unemployment was high in Canada and many volunteers signed up so they could have work that provided them with food, clothing, training and housing.

Frank was given permission to seek work in Toronto where jobs awaited eager workers. His initial employment was in a meat-canning factory. Wartime orders of canned beef and other specialties significantly expanded their work force, as food was being shipped overseas to England and France. It was an interesting time to be living and working in Toronto, as the city was a beehive of activity. Life had meaning, as everyone was working for a cause. It was exhilarating for Frank. He continued painting and studying in his spare time, but foremost in his mind was the determination to enlist and go overseas.

Sean received word that Squire Morris, James's father, and other members of their family were moving to Applewood. Sean and his family were welcome to stay, but Sean knew it was time for them to leave. The mill was running successfully, staffed by experts, and he felt that he had accomplished what he'd been hired to do. The war only accentuated the fact that his children's lives were changing.

Dr. Mack learned through friends that the position of chief of police was open in Whitby, as the acting chief was joining the army. Sean immediately applied for the job and was contacted to come for an interview. His reputation was impeccable and the letters of reference he presented, from James and Dr. Mack, were invaluable. The men who interviewed him didn't seem to worry that he was not an active policeman. So many of their officers were leaving to 'sign up' that their force was depleting at an alarming rate. They needed someone who had the ability to round up a new group of men and Sean was the successful candidate.

Chapter
Twenty-Five

Sean was impressed by the natural beauty of the countryside around Whitby. The proximity to Lake Ontario was a positive factor in his decision making. He returned home to discuss his plans with Maggie and the others, but his mind was already made up. He believed this unforeseen opportunity was meant to be. Everyone had mixed emotions. Applewood felt like their home, but Sean knew their lives were all going to change very soon. He explained this to them, stressing the fact that this home and property was going to feel different when the actual owners arrived. Changes had already made their family smaller.

Spirits lifted as they prepared to leave. They owned very little furniture and few household items. When moving day dawned, a few tears were shed when they said goodbye to James, Dr. Mack and Elizabeth, but the mood changed as they headed for their new home.

Through his friends, Dr. Mack had made arrangements for them to rent a lovely farmhouse, named Greenwood, in Whitby. The original owner was very successful, but as his children grew up, none of them stayed to work the farm. They were lured away toward Toronto for their education. The owner had gradually sold off large parcels of land, then leased the few remaining acres to his neighbours, who farmed it for him.

Before his death, his final instructions to his executors were to rent or sell the house, along with all of the furnishings and contents, 'as the executors saw fit.' The timing was perfect for Sean and Maggie. They preferred to rent it initially since times were unsettled, and this was readily agreed upon by the executors. The house and property would be cared for instead of being left empty and vulnerable. Years later, these words were written in a letter Maeve sent to her niece.

"Greenwood was like a fairyland to me...a huge place sitting on a whole block of land surrounded by lilac bushes. It was fully furnished...great Victorian beds, leather couches, even in the bedrooms. There were so many rooms, twenty-six in all. As we drove up the long, sloping driveway the first time, the chestnut tree was in full bloom. I immediately named it 'the tree with the thousand candles.' Later, as we played chess and read, sitting around that tree, on one of his visits, Frank showed me prints like a horse's hoofs on the back lawn. We were teenagers, but we still skipped, played ball, ran and chased one another. Frank's words were memorable... they inspired me to write my fairy poem, which I still think is good..."

Once again the family settled into a routine. Maggie adjusted well to the move to Greenwood. Sean planted a productive vegetable garden, assisted by the girls. Summer passed happily, even though war was on everyone's mind. Frank joined the reserves and trained with them in Toronto. This heightened his enthusiasm to enlist as soon as he became 'of age.' At seventeen, he didn't have long to wait.

Chapter
Twenty-Six

Alicia met a young man at one of their church suppers. Arthur had been studying at the University in Toronto with plans to become an electrical engineer, but he had recently enlisted and was working at a nearby camp, training the new recruits. Certified as a physical fitness instructor, he had an important role, as the soldiers needed specific training to be physically strong enough to persevere under fire, walk long distances, dig ditches, carry heavy packs, as well as move quickly and efficiently when necessary. Their mental strength depended on their physical strength and vice versa. The recruits almost hated him at times, as he pushed them to their limits, but, once they were overseas, they recalled him with admiration, fondness and sincere appreciation.

Whenever Arthur was given a short leave, he headed for Whitby. Everyone became fond of this tall, quiet man. He enjoyed fishing and often rose before the sun, took his rod and went off, arriving home mid-morning with enough fresh fish for their evening meal. It was obvious that he and Alicia were serious about each other. One evening, Arthur asked to speak with Sean and Maggie. He took Alicia's hand and the four of them walked into the library together.

"Well, Alicia, do you and Arthur wish to hear your mother's and my opinion regarding the tasty fish he gifts us with?" Sean chuckled as he spoke.

Alicia smiled, replying, "This meeting is Arthur's idea, Dad, so he's the spokesman tonight." The two of them sat on the couch, still holding hands.

Without further ado, Arthur spoke, "I'm asking you for permission to marry Alicia. We've known each other for almost a year now and, with your blessings, I'd like to spend my life with this girl. In fact, I love her. She agrees with the whole plan. Right, dear?"

His request did not surprise either Maggie or Sean. They approved of this stable, hard-working young man. Sean looked at Arthur, then replied, "You have our permission and our blessing. Maggie and I have talked about this possibility." Nodding her head, Maggie agreed and asked them when and where they planned to be married.

Smiling, Arthur replied, "Thank you. This might come as a shock to you, but Alicia and I hope to marry this fall. I might be sent overseas in the very near future. We've looked at houses in Toronto. I thought of purchasing one for us, but Alicia has other ideas."

Alicia smiled as she hugged her parents. "Thanks for your approval, Mom and Dad. As Arthur says, we have looked at houses, but I believe that, if he is sent away, my place is here. I can help with the household responsibilities, as well as keep myself from getting too lonesome."

Maggie spoke softly. "We've not forgotten what it's like to be young and in love, have we, Sean? I can understand your wishes to marry soon. Especially during these unsettled times. We could suggest that you wait until after the war, but I believe you've talked everything through. It won't be easy for you to accept the idea of separation. Tell us what kind of wedding you want and we'll all have something happy to plan."

Alicia replied, "I knew you'd both understand. Arthur's next leave is the last weekend in September, so let's set the date right now."

They talked for a while, then went to share their future plans with the others. Congratulations and hugs were given and, shortly after that, Arthur had to leave. He shook hands with Sean and fondly gave Maggie a kiss on the cheek.

With his arm around Alicia's waist, he said, "I love your daughter, this girl of mine, and to the best of my ability, I plan to take good care of her."

The beautiful old house was the scene of happy activity for the following weeks as the forthcoming wedding temporarily took their thoughts away from the war. Alicia put the old sewing machine to good use, as she designed and created her wedding gown of creamy white satin. It was a simple, long, elegant style that flowed from the high neckline to the ground, skimming her slight figure to reveal her tiny waist. She trimmed her mother's lace veil to suit the more modern style of her dress.

Dr. Mack and Elizabeth arrived the night before the wedding. Beth was Alicia's only attendant. She stood beside her sister, wearing the Dresden blue satin gown Alicia had fashioned for her and carrying a bouquet of yellow and white dahlias tied with a bow that matched her dress. Arthur was proud and handsome in his uniform. Elizabeth accompanied Kathleen on the piano as she sang. It was a very special, intimate family occasion.

Two days later, Arthur returned to the training camp while Alicia remained with her family.

Chapter
Twenty-Seven

When Frank came of age the following year, he signed up, was given a condensed training session and soon found himself on a ship travelling from Halifax to England.

The soldiers aboard the ship were enthusiastic and eager to be off to the war. Some of this liveliness was squelched by seasickness, but Frank proved to be one of the fortunate ones who did not suffer from this ailment. Rumours circulated that there were German submarines close by, but their convoy travelled across the Atlantic without incident.

Upon arrival in England, they were sent to a training base near Dover. Long, intensive hours of drills and trench work filled their days. Training was thorough as minds and bodies were honed, preparing these young men for what was yet to come. They knew that battles were raging just across the English Channel, but even the growing casualty lists did not teach them the horrors of war.

Each day, more soldiers arrived for training and others were shipped out. Soon, Frank and his buddies found themselves in France. The second day after his arrival there, Frank faced his first experience of war. They dug in and waited, but not for long. When the shooting erupted, life became a nightmare. There was no time to think clearly. They'd advance, shooting blindly, desperately gaining ground. The order was shouted to 'dig in' again and again. For days on end, they advanced and retreated, never sure if they were winning or losing. Frank wondered if he'd ever be warm and dry again.

When the smoke cleared after each onslaught, they saw that death had come swiftly and viciously as the scene before them revealed war's atrocities. Dismembered, disemboweled bodies lay scattered amidst body parts. A sharp order sent the clean-up crew to swiftly gather up the remains. Identification tags were picked up with other remnants and personal effects. It was a gruesome job for that crew and difficult for the observers to watch. Identification was almost impossible in some cases, but eventually a tally was taken of who was missing. Frank could not help but wonder who would be next. As time went on, the soldiers took the losses for granted as men died with such speed that the ranks were constantly being replaced.

Frank felt a glimmer of pride when he received his officer's commission, but he was realistic, knowing advancements in position came quickly, as losses were high. Deep within the very core of his being, Frank knew that his responsibilities as a leader could prove to be almost unbearable. He decided that, instead of thinking of his men as nameless, fleeting numbers, he'd survive his duties by getting to know them personally, making each man feel special and human, even if only for a few minutes or hours. While they stood side by side serving their country, he'd assure them that they were all here for a common purpose.

During the quiet moments when the guns stopped, the men talked, pouring their hearts out to one another. For a brief span of time, they stretched, tried to relax and breathe deeply and pretended their 'bully beef' staple was a home-cooked chicken dinner. Thoughts of home, their parents, sweethearts, siblings, and pets were shared and these memories kept them going. Quiet, whispered conversations helped to pass the time and eased their constant fear.

A voice came from the darkness beside Frank. "Are you ever frightened, sir? You seem so calm and self-assured."

This was a loaded question, but Frank was prepared. "Of course I'm afraid, Sam. There isn't a man in this area who can't taste fear and smell it. But we're here for a reason. I keep telling myself that. We are here and because we are, just maybe, our families will never have to be exposed to this particular type of hell we are living. By winning these battles, one at a time, we are protecting them. I think of that fact all the time, remembering the nearness of home. It keeps me going and gives me the strength to fight. We are fighting for them."

While trying to reassure this young man, Frank was aware of the silence around him, knowing the others in the trench were listening, straining their ears to hear their conversation. There was silence for a few moments, then Frank spoke again, "This is not easy for any of us, but we must never forget that we are volunteers. Our purpose is self-motivated. We are fighting for our country, our lives and our loved ones. God help us."

Sam spoke again, "My world, our world, has turned into a living hell. I try to take everything in my stride. But when the guns start, I feel physically sick, then I swallow the bitter taste and move and run and duck and shoot like a crazy man. All the time I feel the hate growing inside me. I've never hated like this before. I'm afraid I'm losing my purpose for living. Once, I heard myself screaming, 'Kill them! Kill them! Kill me, you bastards! Get it over with!' Then I hoped and prayed I didn't say this out loud. There was so much noise all around us, I knew it wouldn't matter anyway."

Before Frank could think of a reply, another quiet voice spoke up, "I think about fishing a lot. I'm just a farm boy, you know, from western Canada. Warm summer days after the hoeing is done, I love to go down to the water and fish with my Chesapeake Bay retriever, Red. We spend time there together, just thinking and looking around, feeling at peace with the world. Nature has a way of doing that. Then, when I catch me a fish or two, my happiness is complete. That dog is so funny. He gets bored watching me fish after a while, then he wanders to the narrows and dives for rocks. It's the greatest thing to see! He wades in the water, feels around with his front paws until he locates a certain size of stone. Then he lifts his head, barks and barks, then his head goes under. He comes back up for air, barks again, then under he goes again. Next time his head surfaces, if his tail's wagging, I know he'll have a rock in his mouth. He carries it onto the shore and sets it down. By the end of our time there, he's built a whole pile of rocks! Never taught him to do it, but he sure has skill. You know, that new baby Nance and I have is a boy. He's just a couple of months old and I've never seen him. She sent me a picture and it should come soon. I'll take him fishin' someday when he's big enough. He'll come along with me if we can keep this darn war away from our country. Well, that's about all I can talk about right now. Oh yeah, thanks for listening, guys."

Sam began to complain again and Frank reminded himself that he was an officer. "Enough talk now, men. Get some rest while you can. Courage is easier to find in the morning."

"Hear, hear," another voice whispered.

Peace reigned until dawn was breaking and the barrage of gunfire began again. After several counter-attacks, they were forced to retreat, then once again they moved forward. Minutes slipped by and somehow the sun came up. Occasionally, amidst the din of warfare, a horse whinnied, then screamed in pain. It might have been a human voice.

Sounds blended, shouts carried through a moment of silence. "God help me!" "Where are you, Jim? I can't find you." "Go back, keep low." "Kill them!"

Slowly the smoke cleared once again. Frank's eyes began to focus on images. 'How long will it stay quiet?' he wondered. As if in answer, a gunshot was heard in the distance. Someone was sobbing close by. A voice was swearing. Someone called out for his mother.

"Let's get a head count," he ordered. The men responded and soon realized that many men were missing. Hearing moans close to the trench, Frank climbed out carefully, keeping low to the ground. He worked his way ahead, cautiously crawling on his belly. Finally, he got a hold of someone's foot and carefully dragged him back toward the trench, where reaching arms lifted the wounded soldier into the protected area. Frank moved in beside him and cringed when he saw one leg was missing. The soldier lay face up and part of his face was gone. One eye flickered and Frank moved to hold him in his arms.

"Who is it? Is he dead?" Voices questioned him, but Frank couldn't answer, as he was speaking softly to the dying young man.

A glance at his identification tag revealed that it was Sam. Suddenly he gasped and was gone. He was out of his misery now.

There was work to do and work is a great healer. The wounded were sent by ambulance back to the hospital tents. The bodies were the last to be transported.

Fresh troops of men arrived as replacements. They all looked so neat and tidy in their new uniforms and they seemed so very young. Frank pondered his observation as he thought, *Are they really so young or have we aged?*

They heard a jaunty song being played on a harmonica. A voice said, "Shut up! You'll give our position away."

Another replied, "Let him play. They know where we are. Who do you think they've been shooting at?" A couple of chuckles were heard and the harmonica continued playing.

The Red Cross delivered letters and Frank received a newsy one from Alicia, describing the house Arthur had purchased in Toronto. He'd been sent back from England because of his severe asthma attacks, so he was once again working with the new recruits at the training camp. Frank sighed with relief upon reading this. Alicia had dealt with responsibilities for years and he was pleased that she was finally going to have a life of her own, without the threat of losing her husband in this war.

A letter from his mother described the first snowfall of the season. He closed his eyes and pictured the scene of the landscape changing into a white wonderland. Her words revealed that she was lonesome for him and hoped he'd be coming home soon. She'd been so lost when she sank into that deep depression, but her calm reassurance, sense of fun and dedication toward the family was back. Throughout his life, he and his mom had always been able to talk with each other. He had missed that closeness while she was ill and was grateful that she'd recovered.

Elizabeth wrote to say his art show was a great success. The exhibit was held in a very prestigious studio in Toronto. The event was well attended and the pieces Frank had allowed her to place in the catalogue were sold quickly. Elizabeth was excited to tell him that the portrait of Maggie was chosen as 'Best in Show.' Twelve of his paintings had been shown, along with those of several other young men who were serving overseas. It was a poignant and revealing few days, as the sensitivity and beauty of the paintings reminded people that these talented young artists were off fighting a war for them.

Chapter
Twenty-Eight

On Christmas Eve, in Whitby, the family gathered around the piano to sing carols. Elizabeth and Dr. Mack were staying with them for several days during the Christmas season and were part of the group raising their voices in song. Finishing touches were put on parcels to put under the tree. Soon the big house was in darkness.

Frank was sorely missed. It was difficult to think of him being so far away, across the ocean. Weeks earlier, parcels had been packed with love and mailed to him.

The household was shocked awake in the middle of the night by Beth's sobbing voice. As they rushed from all directions to her room, they found Maeve already there, comforting her sister.

Sean spoke, "What's wrong, Beth? Are you hurt? Did you have a nightmare?"

It took a while to soothe the girl enough to hear what happened. The explanation was a sobering one.

Beth was still breathing heavily as she spoke. "Frank was here. He was standing right over there in his uniform. He looked so hand-some. He had a sash across his chest like this." She used one hand to show the position of the sash. "He told me he loved me and to be a good girl. He sent love to all of you and said goodbye. I ran to him, but he was gone!" She began crying again.

Alicia suggested that they should all go downstairs for some hot chocolate. Once there, she scolded Beth, "You ate too many sweets before going to bed. I told you they'd be upsetting."

They chatted about other things and, after a while, everyone returned to bed. Beth crawled in beside Maeve.

Sean lay awake for a long time. Maggie didn't sleep that night either. She kept picturing her son in his uniform. There was no officer's sash. Beth had never seen one on him, yet how could she describe it so accurately? Slipping out of bed, donning her robe and slippers, she walked over to the window. It was snowing heavily. Her mind was troubled as she watched the snow fall silently, and thought of Frank.

It was strange how the snow could change one's surroundings. Familiar objects and terrain became completely altered. Everything seemed strange, ghostly, and out of proportion. She recalled the last letter she'd sent to Frank, describing the first snowfall of the season. That storm had swept in with a furious, howling wind and lasted for two days. It had taken another two days to clear roads and driveways to get everyone mobile again. They had enjoyed being cooped up in the house together, as it had provided a welcome break in routine. They'd all wished at the time that Kathleen and Frank had been there too. She wondered if Frank had sensed how much he was missed. Probably. They'd all been so close.

Chapter
Twenty-Nine

The day before Christmas dawned peacefully in France. A light dusting of snow fell during the night, mercifully hiding the scarred countryside. Burned out trees, fields gutted by the cruel toys of war, looked strangely white and calm. The soldiers were given the hope of a ceasefire, but in war, nothing was for certain and anything was possible. Morale was low, but letters from home perked the men up.

There were rumours that a sergeant had been shot and killed by one of his own men. When his regiment was questioned, nobody knew anything about the strange, awkward circumstances that led to his death. In this particular incident, there were either no traitors or they were all traitors. It was a well-known fact that this particular man was hated for his unnecessary, bestial treatment of the men beneath him.

"Do you believe he was shot in the back by one of his guys, sir?"

"I don't know. I do believe that, when any man begins to believe he is God because of the uniform he has or the powers he holds, he puts himself in a vulnerable position. No man is better than another because of the clothes he wears, the wealth he has, or the colour of his skin. It's the heart and the brain and the soul that count most. A man's overall integrity. Do you agree?"

This launched a different topic of conversation. Frank had the innate ability to reassure his men by listening to them and still remaining in command. He was famous for the character studies he drew of his men. With a few quick strokes of a charcoal pencil, he could portray an expression, a habit, an attitude, or a tender moment. Many of these sketches had been sent home in letters to loved ones.

Just before the sun set, there was a barrage of fire. It lasted about fifteen minutes. When the smoke cleared, hearts and minds calmed down a bit, but the silence felt ominous. The guns resumed firing and it was obvious they were closer. Retreat was necessary. The men who'd charged ahead scurried back to their trenches while shells exploded in their midst. Frank did a brief nose count, waited until all was quiet, then slipped out of the trench to assist a fallen soldier.

A sniper was waiting. As Frank reached his soldier and slung him over his shoulder, a single shot rang out. Both men fell in a heap. The men were silent as the ambulance corps took the two soldiers away.

Frank's body felt strange. He gasped with pain as they lifted him onto a stretcher, then he felt pleasantly numb. He thought of Alicia, with her spunky nature and her ability to do so many things; Maeve, the student with those lovely blue eyes; Kathleen and her glorious voice; Dorothy, the actress, the renegade; Beth with her strawberry blonde hair, love of books and her sunshine face. Suddenly he felt chilled, then warm, so warm. He felt his heart fluttering. And then it stopped beating.

Chapter
Thirty

Sean lay in bed, listening to the howl of the wind and the steady drum of the rain. He knew it was morning, but he felt lethargic and weary. Several times during the night, he'd wakened from a fitful sleep. His mind kept living and reliving the events of the past few months.

Maggie had succumbed to the influenza epidemic that was running rampant throughout the country. She had taken to her bed with a fever and, within four days, she was gone. Everything had happened so quickly. It was a stunned and saddened family that gathered for her funeral, only three weeks after Frank's memorial service.

During the past few years, Maggie's health had improved. She never quite regained her old vitality and zest for life, but his life companion, dear wife and the mother of his children had once again become his confidante. Her sudden death was like another chapter in a bad dream. The problem was, when he awoke each morning, the nightmare was still with him. Every day, he forced himself to go through the motions of living. He spent time with Dorothy and Beth, the only two remaining at home. He ate his meals. He went to work.

Yesterday, he'd gone with some other police officers to the site of an accident. The scene was a tragic one. Ten teenagers had piled into a pick-up truck to attend a dance only a few miles away. A dense fog crept silently in off the lake. They turned onto the wrong road and plunged down an embankment into Lake Ontario. Four of them were miraculously uninjured and swam to shore. The six in the back of the truck drowned. As he walked along the shore and began climbing back up the hill, he heard a voice say, "Do you suppose he even knows Dorothy was at that dance?"

Without stopping to ask questions, he returned to the car and sat waiting for the other men to return. His whole being was consumed with rage. This was the final straw. He'd occasionally heard someone imply that 'Dorothy is the wild one.' He didn't consider the fact that most of the teenagers attended the dances with their parents' permission. He had not paid much attention to this daughter, who was in her senior year of high school.

Sean returned to the office and worked late, helping the others finalize the accident report. He called their newly hired housekeeper to tell her he'd be late and not to wait dinner. Walking to and from work was a daily routine he enjoyed, but that evening, he slowly returned, hardly noticing anything or anybody along the way. When Greenwood appeared before him, he simply couldn't force himself to go inside.

He turned toward the orchard. Blossoms reflected the moonlight, giving an ethereal beauty to the scene. Once calm gradually returned to his troubled mind, he decided to go in and talk with Dorothy. With a sense of purpose, he entered the house.

Beth sat at the kitchen table doing homework. She looked up as he came in. "Hi, Dad. Would you like a sandwich?"

"No thanks, Beth. I want to see Dorothy. Has she gone upstairs to bed?"

"Yes. She has a headache, so she took a cup of tea and went up about half an hour ago. Can you sit for a moment? I want to tell you a few things about school." Sean hesitated. He was dreading his conversation with Dorothy. Beth's face sparkled with love and enthusiasm. What did it matter if he chatted with her for a while? He sat down, welcoming the cup of hot tea she prepared for him.

The better part of an hour slipped by before he said goodnight and headed up the stairs.

He rapped gently on Dorothy's bedroom door. There was no answer. He knocked again, a little louder. There was still no answer. Turning the knob, he opened the door partway and softly said, "Dorothy, I'm sorry to waken you, but we need to talk. May I please come in?" He pushed the door wide open and stepped into her room.

As his eyes adjusted to the darkness, the gentle rays of moonlight revealed an empty bed. There was no sign of Dorothy. He glanced out her window, toward the sloping roof and the large rose trellis. His gaze followed the line of the grape arbours beyond. Either something moved, or his eyes were playing tricks on him. Perhaps it was a fox, or a coyote searching for food.

Where was Dorothy? How easily he was distracted these days! If the officers were telling the truth, Dorothy must be in the habit of sneaking out at night after he and Beth were settled down. Quickly retracing his footsteps, he walked down the stairs, hoping to see Beth and Dorothy lingering by the fireplace. He was disappointed. Continuing along the hall, checking the parlour and the dining room, he arrived back at the kitchen and sat down.

Since they were now three people living in an empty house, most of the upper areas were shut off, only opened to freshen the air and get rid of the dust. He'd called her name several times. Surely she'd answer if she could hear him. Should he search every room in the house?

He wished he could talk this over with Maggie. The thought of her overwhelmed him. She was gone. Frank was gone. Alicia and Kathleen were in Toronto and Maeve lived in Montreal.

Sean went outside and breathed deeply a few times, pushing his grief back into the furthest corners of his mind.

A quick movement caught his eye once more. He stood up and headed for the arbour. Suddenly, he and Dorothy came face to face. Shock and fear registered on her face. All thought of a calm discussion flew from Sean's mind. He could hear himself shouting at her as she pushed past him and ran for the house. He followed and grabbed for her arm. As she wrenched away, he lifted his hand and slapped her.

"I hate you! I hate you! Leave me alone. You don't even try to understand! You don't hear me anymore!"

Her words shocked him into consciousness, but by this time, she'd raced up the stairs. He heard her bedroom door slam shut. There would be no more communication tonight. Perhaps it was better to sleep and let the problem rest. Slowly, Sean returned to the porch. He felt old and weak and very, very helpless. Had he really hit her? He put his head down and wept. For Maggie, for Frank, for Dorothy, and for himself. His shoulders shook. It was a long time before the tears stopped. Exhausted, he climbed the stairs and went to bed.

Chapter
Thirty-One

Sean wakened to the welcome aroma of coffee. Wearily, he stepped out of bed, then washed and dressed.

Beth was sitting at the table, finishing her breakfast when he walked into the kitchen. Their 'once a week' housekeeper, Patsy, was chatting with her.

Beth grinned at him. "Good morning, sleepyhead! I can't remember ever beating you to the breakfast table." She stood up and hugged him.

Obviously, she hadn't heard the uproar last night. Sean was relieved. This darling girl was always so relaxed and easy with him. He watched as the smile faded from Beth's face. She realized he hadn't answered and noted that his face looked haggard and grey.

"Are you sick, Dad? I should have remembered about the accident. Were many of the kids hurt? They didn't say much at school yesterday, as they were awaiting news from the police."

"No Beth, I'm not ill. Just upset about things and I didn't sleep well. Where is Dorothy? Isn't she down yet?"

Patsy spoke up, "I was just going to ask Beth to run up and fetch her. If she doesn't hurry up, she'll be late for school. Please tell her to 'shake a leg,' Beth."

Beth returned with a puzzled look on her face. "She isn't there, Dad, but there were notes on her pillow. This one's for me. She left other notes addressed to Alicia and Arthur, Maeve, Kathleen, as well as to Elizabeth and Dr. Mack.

Beth opened her letter, read it silently to herself, and then handed it to her father.

"Dear Beth,

I am writing this note to you because I feel you are the only family member left in this house who cares enough about me to deserve an explanation.

As you know, Jim and I have been going steady for quite a while. His mother doesn't approve of me and Dad doesn't even know he exists. We are leaving together. Please don't worry. We are going somewhere to be married right away. We're both ambitious, strong and healthy. I know we can soon find jobs. I will send you my address later, when I have one.

Love,

Dorothy"

They sat in silence as Sean read the note to himself, then set it down.

"Beth, you'd better hurry or you'll be late for school. Please keep this to yourself. News will get around soon enough."

He looked down as her hand covered his. "Dad, I'm not going to school today and you are missing work. We have a few things we must do together. First, we'll visit the bus station, then Jim's parents. Oh yes, we'll drop by the police station and the school to let them know not to expect either of us today."

When had his little Beth grown up? She was taking control of the situation and he felt relieved. Nodding his head, he replied, "Thanks, Beth. You are obviously thinking more clearly than I am."

Soon they were in the car. Beth talked to him as they drove along. "Dorothy will probably not be easy to find, Dad. She's not a bad girl, just full of ambition and energy. Did you know she taught herself to type during spare classes at school? She has even done extra typing projects for the principal. She's very clever. Our teachers all like her."

She continued, saying that she'd often discussed her concerns for Dorothy with Alicia and Arthur. Throughout the years, Alicia had often tried to talk with her younger, rebellious sister. Unfortunately,

Dorothy was impetuous and defiant toward her father. When Alicia suggested that Dorothy should communicate with him, she laughed and told Alicia to mind her own business.

Frank's death, followed so soon by her mother's passing, made Dorothy even more reticent about trying to tell Sean she was in love. What did he know or care about things like that?

Now she was gone and Beth was not surprised. Could she have prevented Dorothy from leaving? She doubted it. In her heart, she believed that her interference would only have made the situation worse.

"Dad, I must tell you that she has taken some of her clothes. Obviously, Jim helped her. He is a nice person. I think they do love each other."

Sean sighed. Clearly, this was pre-planned and last night's upset had brought everything to a head. When they reached the police station, he spoke privately with his deputy chief. The two men had become friends and Mark Beatty listened to Sean with a compassionate heart. "I'll take care of things here, Chief. Do what you have to do."

Beth ran into the school and told the principal she had to miss school for family reasons. Then they drove to the bus station, located at the general store. Mr. Hanes, the proprietor, was a diligent worker who ran his store, sold bus tickets and supervised the post office. "Good morning! Help yourself. I'll be out in a jiffy."

Sean followed his voice to the back of the store. Mr. Hanes saw him approaching and climbed down from the ladder he was using to reach the higher shelves.

"Chief Sean, mornin' to you and to the young lady too. Say, that was some tragic accident, wasn't it? My boy was at that dance, and the Missus and I just feel so thankful that he rode his bike there before the fog set in. Otherwise he might've been with them. Why they were all friends. Terrible thing. That old road should have been blocked off."

Without answering, Sean nodded his head. "Mr. Hanes, were there any buses scheduled to go through here bound for Toronto this morning?"

"Well, one went by about an hour ago, but there weren't any passengers here, so the driver only slowed down long enough to toss out a parcel for Mrs. Red."

"How about during the night?"

"Nope, there just isn't any call for one then. What are you after, Sean, a bank robber? Something been going on I don't know about?"

Sean thought for a moment. "No, just curious. Can a person board the bus without buying a ticket?"

"Well sure, sometimes the folks outside town flag him down. Saves them coming all the way into the store. He sells them a ticket right on the bus."

They passed the time of day for a few minutes longer, then Sean and Beth left the store. Beth wanted to ask more about the accident, but the timing didn't seem right. She had heard at school yesterday that it was very serious. They drove in silence until Sean spoke. "Where do Jim's parents live, Beth?"

She directed her father to their house. Sean recalled Dorothy's note saying that Jim's mother didn't approve of her. He frowned, as he found that statement to be very annoying. Even though he was upset with Dorothy, he realized that feeling protective toward her, in the face of anyone else's disapproval, was a good sign.

"Dad, I want to come in with you, please." Beth opened her door as she spoke.

Sean paused, then said, "Okay, Beth. I guess this was your idea, wasn't it?"

He used the impressive door knocker to announce their arrival. The door was answered by a very proper, rigid butler. "Whom may I say is calling, sir?"

"Well now, William, you know me," Sean replied. *He should know me,* he thought to himself. *We've kept him in jail overnight a few times when he's had a day off.*

Poor William was unable to control his liquor when he was off work, or on a holiday.

"Yes, Chief MacGrotty. I didn't recognize you without your uniform." Flustered, the poor fellow opened the door and offered to take their coats and the umbrella, and then announced their presence to someone in the library.

Mrs. Snow soon faced them in the hall. "That will be all, William." She was obviously very distraught.

"Good morning, Mrs. Snow. I don't believe we've met. I am Dorothy's father, Sean MacGrotty, and this is my daughter, Beth."

She rudely ignored his out-stretched hand, saying, "I know who you are. Why are you here? They've gone and that should make you happy. She got exactly what she wanted. My son. The no good…" She stopped mid-sentence as she saw the look in Sean's eyes.

He interrupted her before she could say any more. "I am not here to accuse you or your son of anything. Dorothy is gone. She left a note. Your son is quite a bit older than her, as she's not eighteen yet. Do you know where they've gone?"

The way he emphasized 'quite a bit' alarmed Mrs. Snow. She blamed Dorothy, but hearing she was underage suddenly made Jim responsible. Her face crumpled and she dabbed at her eyes with a handkerchief. Her tone of voice was not as officious as she spoke. "Please come into the drawing room. I'm so upset, I've forgotten my manners."

With that comment, she turned and led them into a very elegant room. Ordinarily, Sean might have commented on the exquisite taste and beauty of the decor. Today, he had other, more important things on his mind.

"Do you wish any coffee or tea?" she asked, trying to restore a sense of dignity to the scene.

"No, thank you. I do appreciate your offer, but to be blunt, I'm very worried about my daughter. If you are aware of their destination, please tell me immediately. I have no time for formalities. I beg of you, Mrs. Snow, tell me what you know."

"I do not have any idea. Milton, my husband, found out this morning that Jim has been drawing his savings from the bank bit by bit. No one even thought to inform us, as Jim is old enough to manage his own financial matters. They took for granted that he was making an investment. His car is gone. He left a note saying they were eloping and that the car can be picked up by Milton in Toronto." After this statement, she burst into uncontrollable weeping.

"Do you have the address of the car lot in Toronto?"

Wordlessly, she handed him a piece of paper. Sean nodded his head and they left.

As they walked down the front walk, a voice called out to him. "Sean MacGrotty, wait a moment."

Sean stood still and waited. A tall, well-dressed man was coming toward them from the side of the house. He shook hands as he spoke. "I am Milton Snow, Jim's father. We've never met before. And who is this young lady?"

Sean introduced Beth and Milton continued speaking. "My son, Edward, and I are driving into Toronto today. Would you like to come with us?"

Relieved, Sean answered truthfully. "Thank you. We most certainly would. I'm planning on going there myself and this will save me the bother of finding transportation. I can't very well take the police car since I'm not certain how long I'll be gone. If you don't mind, Beth will come too."

Beth and Sean returned home, packed a few articles of clothing and, within the hour, Milton Snow picked them up and they were on their way. The situation was a sensitive subject and, for once, Sean was at a loss for words.

Milton broke the silence. "My son has not done the right thing, running away with a girl of Dorothy's age. He's been obsessed with her for quite a while now. We should have paid more attention. I truly believe he loves her, Sean, if that's any comfort to you. She's a delightful girl. So bright and intelligent, full of fun and beautiful. Jim's a quiet lad and she has added zest to his life. I'm sure you realize the war has changed things for all of us. So many young people have died. It has made our children bolder and who's to say they're wrong?"

He stopped talking, then said softly, "Please accept my sincere sympathy for the loss of your son and your wife. And now this." His voice trailed away.

Sean sat thinking his own thoughts before he replied. "I appreciate your kindness. This has been a sad time for our family. Sometimes, it feels as if everything happened ages ago. Right now, I feel as if it were yesterday. I do hope we find those two before they do anything too foolish. Really, they're both so young."

When they arrived in the outskirts of Toronto, Milton turned toward Sean. "Do you want to come to the car lot with us? You can use that vehicle while you're here and drive it back when you return to Whitby."

Sean observed this very kind man, who was trying desperately to ease the awkward situation for all of them. With stiff Irish pride, he answered, "Believe me, I will never forget the kindness you have shown to Beth and to me today. I plan to visit my daughter, Kathleen, who lives and works here, and to take Beth to stay with my other daughter, Alicia. I must decline your offer for two reasons. I'm a stubborn old rascal, and I simply do not know you well enough to accept your offer. The other reason is far more logical. I plan to look for Dorothy and Jim. If they have left Toronto, I intend to find out where they've gone, so I'm not sure when I will return to Whitby. You are, indeed, a gentleman and I do thank you again, Milton, but please, just let us out anywhere along here." He tipped his hat at Milton, opened the door for Beth, retrieved their valises and walked away. In each of their hearts, these two men, the fathers of the runaways, carried the desire to meet one another again under different circumstances.

Chapter
Thirty-Two

Upon her arrival home from work, Kathleen was surprised to see her father and sister sitting on a bench in front of her boarding house, waiting for her.

"Dad! Beth! What a pleasant surprise! What are you doing here? I didn't dream you'd ever just come to see me like this. Will you have dinner here tonight? Mrs. Manley won't mind. She enjoys having visitors, especially men!"

Realizing too late how that sounded, she laughed nervously and changed her statement. "What I mean is, she misses her husband, so she loves to hear a man's voice around the house. Oh, I'm so delighted to see you both!"

Her voice had a lovely lilt. She sounded happy and Sean held off telling her the reason for their unannounced visit. Perhaps he'd wait and see if she mentioned seeing Dorothy, but anxiety won. He asked her, "Kathleen, have you seen or heard from Dorothy today?"

"No, Dad. Didn't she come to the city with you? I know she wants to find work here, but she plans to finish school first. This is a school day, isn't it?"

Sean told his daughter a brief version of what had happened. He kept taking deep breaths, trying to strengthen his voice, which sounded strangely tense and weak. He sighed as he finished speaking.

Beth spoke up. "Kathleen, she left this note for you."

Kathleen took the envelope from her, opened it and read the contents. Speechless, she reached for her father's hand and gave it a gentle squeeze. She moved their overnight bags inside the house, wrote a note to Mrs. Manley and came back down the front steps.

"Your bags will be fine there. We're going to visit my favourite tea shop. It's a short walk from here."

Slipping one arm through Sean's and one through Beth's, Kathleen led them away from the boarding house and down the street, toward a small tea shop a block away. She tried to collect her thoughts, so her words might help alleviate her father's obvious pain. He had suffered so much. How could Dorothy do such a thing?

They were soon seated at a corner table near a window.

"You make this sound as if it's the end of the world, Dad. It isn't, you know. Jim loves Dorothy. He'll care for her. She was always like a caged bird in our family, restless and eager and so full of life. Actually, most of the time, she is so much fun! Didn't you realize she wasn't happy with us? We've had such awful fights. She has her own way of doing things, and was constantly antagonizing us. I guess we fought mostly when you weren't around. Alicia handled her with bribes. Maybe I'm speaking out of turn, but there does come a time when you have to leave. Dad, she's young, but believe me, she's ready. I think you should stop blaming yourself for the things we do, simply because they don't please you. You've encouraged each one of us to study and learn to be self-sufficient. I agree with you. Look at us! Alicia, Maeve and I are each independent in our own way. Our family has suffered, but you've given us backbones. Dorothy will make her way in the world. Just wait and see."

Sean listened to Kathleen. Her words rang with passion and truth. His anger had left him feeling defenceless and unsure of himself. How could he possibly tell his daughters that he'd slapped Dorothy last night? He'd tried to be a good father to his family. Should a parent feel guilty when a child goes astray? He loved each one of them, but he had his favourites. Was that wrong? Wasn't it normal for certain personalities to clash while others were easy to have around? For an odd moment, he felt as if Kathleen had read his mind, then wondered if he'd spoken aloud. Regardless, she made good sense.

They sat and enjoyed their tea. It was a pretty place, full of sunshine and light, conversation and music, old china, and perfect scones served with butter, jam and a pot of special, thick cream. Sean had not eaten all day, and strangely, he was actually hungry. When they left to walk back to Kathleen's place, their steps seemed lighter.

Mrs. Manley met them at the door of her boarding house. As Kathleen had predicted, she was delighted to see Beth and Sean.

"Well, I hope you didn't spoil your supper. As I always say, afternoon tea is meant to tide you over to your next meal. Now I have to leave you, as I have a few preparations to begin for later. If you plan to spend the night, there's a comfortable cot in Kathleen's room for you, young lady, and another empty room all freshly made up for you, Mr. MacGrotty. It is a real coincidence. That room was vacated yesterday and I don't have another boarder coming for two days!" She bustled off, leaving Kathleen to show them around.

"Dad, will you and Beth stay the night? I didn't realize she had a vacant room, but it will be wonderful to have you both here."

Before Sean answered, Mrs. Manley reappeared. "Did Kathleen tell you she sings in the choir at the Presbyterian Church? They're so thrilled to have her. With that lovely voice, she's made us the envy of a few other churches. Last week, she sang at a special tea dance, put on by a women's organization that sends parcels to our boys overseas. It was a great success. Some of the women asked Kathleen if she'd sing at other events. I've told her she has enough talent to make a living by singing, but she says it's her hobby. Hobby my eye! This girl has a God-given talent." With that comment, she excused herself again and returned to the kitchen.

Sean found himself smiling as she left the room. "Well, my girl, it seems as if you've been taken right under milady's wing. It's very homey here, isn't it?"

Then and there, he decided they'd accept her offer and stay the night. Tomorrow was another day and it was too late to upset Alicia and Arthur.

They sat together in the parlour before dinner as tempting aromas wafted through the air. Sean's tension eased and he felt himself relaxing, even though his determination to locate Dorothy was not abandoned. Meanwhile, he'd given Kathleen's address to Milton Snow. Until he heard from him, he might as well be patient. If the car was indeed found in the specified parking lot, Jim might have left another note for his father, hopefully revealing their destination. If so, Sean planned to check bus and train schedules and to follow the young couple, so he could talk some sense into their heads. Until those facts were known, he'd simply be on a wild goose chase.

Later that evening, a letter was delivered to Sean in care of Kathleen. It was from Milton Snow. He informed Sean that the car was found exactly where Jim said it would be. He also mentioned that Jim had left a second note, stating that he and Dorothy were planning their marriage as soon as it could be arranged. They were leaving the country and would not appreciate being followed.

Sean handed the letter to Kathleen. She read it, handed it to Beth, and then turned to her father, saying, "Dad, don't go. If you follow them, it will make matters worse. Please think about this. You probably won't find them anyway."

Her father didn't answer. Later in the evening, Mrs. Manley played the piano as Kathleen sang. Beth, Sean and two of the other boarders joined in a sing-song.

Sean thought about things. *When morning comes, Beth and I will visit Alicia and tell her about Dorothy. Then I'll make my decision. That will be soon enough.*

Chapter
Thirty-Three

A few weeks later, Kathleen stood looking out the window of her room. She was used to rising early to get to work on time. Now she had a few days off and it was difficult to sleep in. The sky was tinted a rosy glow of pink, the soft colour of sweet peas. Slowly, the sun peeked over the horizon, sending rays of light in all directions. A new day was born.

Would she ever get over the absolute joy she felt watching the sun rise? She hoped not. Watching a grey sliver of cloud slip across the sun, followed by a threatening dark cloud, she knew the weatherman had been correct after all when he predicted showers. She turned from the window, feeling rather smug and happy, wondering how many people would miss this morning's sun.

She turned from the window, thinking about this most unusual spring. Her father had not been content to allow Dorothy to leave home, without at least trying to find her. Believing he could encourage Jim and Dorothy to return home, he had followed one clue after another, only to be disappointed in the end. It was sad to watch him. One lead that he received from a bus driver sent him off to Quebec for two weeks. When he finally found the couple who closely fit his description of Dorothy and Jim, he was elated. The moment the door of their home opened, he was disheartened. They were not Dorothy and Jim! Embarrassed, he introduced himself to the married couple who spoke French and only understood a few English words. They listened to his explanations, then wished him well. A sad, disillusioned Sean headed back to Toronto empty-handed.

One Saturday evening, Mrs. Manley invited him to attend church with Kathleen and her the next day. As he walked into the impressive stone building, passing slowly through the beautiful, carved wooden doors, he saw the stained glass windows capturing the sun's rays, sending dancing prisms of light throughout the church. The music from a huge pipe organ swelled his heart almost to the bursting point as the instrument was played by a maestro. He was glad he'd come. Somehow the joys and the sorrows of his life were reflected in that music.

Kathleen's solo added a special touch to the service as her voice, combining power and sweetness, soared through the air, bringing tears to his eyes. He was so proud of her. Once again, as the magnificent chords from the organ fell upon his ears, there seemed to be a harmony to life. He had not felt this way for a long, long time. Sean listened to the sermon, but afterwards, he couldn't recall the theme. Just the music. Music that had gifted him with the peace and comfort he'd been seeking.

After church, he took Beth, Kathleen and Mrs. Manley to supper in one of the better hotels. When they finished eating, the weather had cleared enough for them to walk down by the lake. The water reflected the grey of the sky, and the ominous, black clouds hovering on the horizon promised more rain. The wind was gentle as they strolled, breathing in the fresh air that carried the scents of spring.

Sean remained in Toronto for another month. He went on two more searches after receiving some very promising clues. The most upsetting one came to his attention quite by accident. Making his regular rounds at the bus and the train stations, he approached the wicket asking his usual question, making a point of describing Dorothy. The woman working there proceeded to ask him if the man Dorothy was with was tall, with a moustache. Sean realized he'd not even mentioned Jim and that he didn't even know whether he had a moustache. On a hunch, he nodded his head.

"Did she have a sporty, bright red coat?" Again he nodded his head.

"Well, I didn't have a job here yet, but I'd bought a train ticket, as I was going to visit my grandmother. This friendly couple travelled as far as Windsor with me. They were great fun and asked for my address in Toronto, promising they'd write to me when they arrived and had a permanent address. They seemed the type to keep their word. I believe they'll drop me a note someday. They were newlyweds and were spending their honeymoon at a boarding house in Windsor."

Sean's hand trembled as he handed her Kathleen's address, asking her to contact Kathleen if she heard from them. He thanked her, purchased a train ticket to Windsor and left the station to pack his bag. He told Mrs. Manley and Kathleen that he was going away for a few days.

His mind wandered as he rode on the train bound for Windsor. He recalled the day that Dorothy had arrived home, wearing that new red coat. Alicia was visiting them in Whitby at the time. Dorothy had bounced into the kitchen looking very smartly dressed, twirled around and showed it off with a smile. He had reacted negatively, telling her she seemed too old and too flashy in it. Surprised and saddened by her father's disapproval, she left the room and went upstairs. The slam of her bedroom door angered him. Dorothy felt hurt and disappointed, but she was also stubborn enough to totally ignore him when she returned downstairs for dinner.

Looking at her, Sean had realized with a start that it wasn't only the coat that made her look older. It was her hair! She'd had it bobbed! All that beautiful, fair hair cut off. For a whim! He had opened his mouth to reprimand her, but a look from Alicia stopped him mid-sentence.

Later that evening, she took her father aside. "Dad, Dorothy's new hairstyle is perfect for her. It's simply ridiculous that women have to wear their hair long. This style suits her and it's the most sensible decision women have made in years! Don't be surprised if we all get our hair cut. I do believe you're letting yourself become very old-fashioned and set in your ways." And that was that.

Sean was thunderstruck. Alicia was his refuge and a shoulder to lean on. It had shocked him to hear her taking him to task. But it did the trick. He calmed down and regarded her with a twinkle in his eye. "Don't be getting yours cut off, Alicia. Arthur loves the way you wear it."

She tossed her head and replied tartly, "I just might get it chopped off after this baby arrives. Now that I live in the city, the summers seem much hotter. Surely, it's me Arthur loves, not this head of hair!"

They both burst out laughing. She'd given her father a few thoughts to ponder, but after Alicia returned to her home in Toronto, the gap between Dorothy and himself widened.

Returning to the present, Sean stared out the window of the train, fruitlessly wishing he could somehow keep the good memories and re-do the sad ones. He fell asleep, wakening with a start when the conductor announced that Windsor was the next stop.

He stayed in a local hotel, then spent four days visiting boarding houses, one by one. Finally, he found the one he was looking for.

A pleasant woman appeared from the back of the house when he rang the desk bell. She removed her apron as she greeted him and Sean briefly revealed his reason for being there.

With a smile, she responded, "Why yes, Mr. and Mrs. Snow stayed with us for two nights. They were heading for California. Excited they were too. They promised to send us a line when they arrived there. Look what came in the post yesterday! A pretty postcard from them! We save the ones we receive from guests who travel all over. See? You can read it. They don't have a set address yet, but they'll keep in touch." Noting the concern on Sean's face, she added, "Oh dear, I hope everything is all right with your family. She spoke so fondly of her sisters."

Sean listened in a daze. So far away. No address. He thanked the proprietor and left, already planning his next move. After purchasing a ticket for the next train to Toronto, he settled into his seat, feeling mentally and physically exhausted as he returned to the city he'd left a few days ago with such high hopes. Looking out the window, he listlessly watched the scenes flash by. Tiny houses were clustered comfortably near the tracks; washing hung on clotheslines; children waved at the train; farmers ploughed the fields, their steady hands guiding the sturdy horses; dogs chased the train. Life was moving steadily on as people faced their futures one day at a time. He must do the same.

Chapter
Thirty-Four

Beth was now living with Alicia and Arthur. They'd welcomed her with open arms. Alicia had been a 'mother figure' to her youngest sister throughout all the moves and the troubled years. Beth finished her last two months of secondary school in Toronto, then applied and was accepted to attend Normal School there. Her dream was happening, as she'd always wanted to be a teacher, like Elizabeth.

Facing the fact that he'd neglected his other duties to search for Dorothy, Sean returned to Whitby. The house felt lifeless and empty with everyone gone. The furnishings sat like silent ghosts, wrapped in their white dust coverings. Sean had come back to tie up loose ends. He asked to be relieved from his position as chief of police. The deputy chief had willingly filled in for Sean while he was gone and he'd missed him as his boss, as well as his friend. However, he was quite pleased to know that he would be promoted to chief.

Sean signed the papers that cancelled his rental agreement. The present owners planned to sell the house and property to buyers who were turning it into a luxury hotel. It was easy for Sean to pack up his few personal belongings and leave.

Mrs. Manley was delighted when he returned to Toronto, secretly hoping his short stay would become more than a temporary home. She knew why he was leaving Whitby and her heart ached for him. He and his family had certainly had more than their share of sadness and tragedy. She was a good listener, so it was easy for Sean to confide in her. He planned to stay there for two weeks before widening his search, but summer and fall slipped by as he secretly planned the next stage of his life.

Beth remained with Alicia and Arthur. She willingly helped her sister with household chores and was delighted to hear their first baby was due late in the fall.

Sean and Milton Snow met for dinner several times throughout the summer and fall. Initially, their common bond encouraged them to keep in touch. It was a strange feeling, knowing their children had run away from them. Gradually, they became friends, as respect and common interests drew them closer to each other. At times, they'd be discussing a variety of subjects, then one or the other would suddenly realize they hadn't even mentioned the names of their runaways. Dorothy and Jim had not contacted anyone.

It was during the quiet times, when he was alone, that Sean thought of Dorothy. He continued to blame himself for allowing their communication to totally break down. Thankfully, Alicia, Beth and Kathleen gradually convinced him that Dorothy was her own person and had been for years. She was born to pursue her own path, regardless of anyone else. Maeve's letters expressed the same opinion and, eventually, Sean began to believe them. As time passed, he became less critical of himself.

Life brought changes. He was a survivor and he often recalled one of Dr. Mack's sayings, "Survivors do not sink; they swim."

Chapter
Thirty-Five

Sean arrived at Alicia and Arthur's house one snowy afternoon in December. He'd spent the morning shopping for Christmas gifts and his car was laden with parcels to put under their tree. There was a hint of snow in the air and Christmas was only three weeks away. Alicia's baby was due any day. She'd greeted him at the front door and insisted on holding it open as he and the driver made several trips from the carriage he'd rented, carrying the gifts inside.

When everything was unloaded, he removed his coat, hat and overshoes in the front vestibule. Alicia smiled as she watched her father. His enthusiasm was so obvious. She spoke as she hugged him. "Dad, what a lovely surprise! I'll make us a pot of tea to warm you up, and you go ahead and place everything under the tree. Just place them wherever you please."

A few days earlier, Arthur had taken Alicia and Beth for a drive to a woods north of the city. They soon realized he'd planned the after-noon and was well-prepared. Arthur chopped the chosen Christmas tree down with an axe and tied it securely onto the top of the car for the trip home. Following Alicia's directions, he set it up in a corner of their house, right between the living area and the dining room. That evening he, Alicia and Beth trimmed the tree with strings of popcorn they'd made, candy canes and other decorations.

As Sean set each gift under Alicia and Arthur's tree, he felt happy and full of anticipation, and he pondered each tagged parcel, knowing exactly what it held. There was a wonderful spinning top for his expected grandchild; an up-to-date sewing machine for Alicia; a new pair of skates and a hockey stick for Beth; a fancy cigarette rolling gadget, complete with tobacco and papers for Arthur; a blue sweater and hat for Maeve; season's tickets to the symphony and a cape for Kathleen; and a box of specialty chocolates and a pair of fine leather gloves for Mrs. Manley. He hung a new collar for Ben, the beagle, on one of the lowest branches. Tucked inside each of his daughters' gifts was a piece of Maggie's jewellery. Elizabeth and Mack were coming from their home north of Toronto to join them for Christmas dinner. One of their packages held Maggie's pearls, the other a specialty pipe and tobacco.

Two weeks before Christmas, Alicia's baby girl was born at Toronto General Hospital. Their household seemed even homier with the presence of their new baby, Margaret Renee. When they arrived home from the hospital, Arthur insisted that Alicia curl up on the couch to rest. He made a pot of tea and served it with a few slices of the date and nut loaf that Alicia had made a few weeks before. They sat together quietly, treasuring the moment. When the baby stirred, Arthur held her in his arms and greeted her. "You take after your mom, love. With that head of dark hair and very fair skin, we'll know who you belong to." He carried her around the inside of their house talking to her, pointing out their bedroom and the one she'd eventually have for her very own. Father and daughter bonded from that moment on.

School, homework and hockey games had kept Beth busy during the autumn months, but she had anticipated the birth of the new baby eagerly. Beth loved her tiny niece from the first moment she set eyes on her. Sometimes she simply stood by the bassinet and watched Renee sleep. Her older sister had been a solid and friendly mother figure, as well as a loving sister, throughout her life. Now Alicia had her own baby and everything seemed so right. Beth was a useful presence around the household as she changed Renee's diapers, rocked and sang to her.

Even the puppy welcomed the new baby. Alicia insisted, from the day Arthur had brought Ben home, that he should be trained so he could roam through their home all day long, but he was to sleep in the back entrance at night. Then she proceeded to make a cozy bed for him. Nobody had argued with her. Not even the dog.

When baby Renee arrived home, Alicia allowed Ben to inspect her from head to toe. From then on, each time she was placed gently in the bassinet to sleep, he took his daytime naps lying underneath. Arthur commented with a smile, "See girls? I told you. Babies and beagles are meant to be together!"

Christmas Day dawned. It was a sunny, frosty cold day, but there was nothing cool about the gathering that was held in the little duplex on Webb Avenue. Beth and Arthur had prepared the dressing and stuffed it into the turkey early in the morning. Alicia was 'queen for the day' and she wasn't allowed to lift a finger toward the dinner. They joined hands as they sat around the table and bowed their heads in prayer as Dr. Mack said the Grace. "Bless this food to our use and us to Thy purpose. Bless each one gathered around this table. Keep the new baby safe. We give thanks with mindful hearts. Let us remember the loved ones who are no longer with us. Amen." Their numbers had dwindled, but their hearts felt blessed and happy.

When the turkey and all the trimmings were eaten, the leftovers doled out into neat packages, and the kitchen tidied, the kettle was put on to make tea.

As they sipped tea and ate Alicia's famous carrot pudding served with hot rum sauce, Sean shared his news.

He had purchased a small vineyard and winery in California. There was a stunned silence, then Beth spoke, "Really, I'm not surprised, Dad. Our lives have all changed so much. Tell us more about your plans. I can't believe you're going all the way to California!"

His enthused voice explained that, while reading a newspaper, he happened to notice a 'Land for Sale: California' advertisement. It sounded interesting. He had sent an initial letter of inquiry and soon letters flowed back and forth. He hired a lawyer to read everything over before signing the papers. Then both of them visited his bank and official transactions were conducted.

Opening a small valise, Sean produced copies of his ownership document, several photos of the property and a signed description of the acreage which included the vineyards, the house, several out-buildings and the winery. He passed the photos around and questions flew at him from every direction. Obviously, everyone was surprised, but they seemed excited for him. Perhaps they silently wondered how on earth he'd kept such a life-changing secret from all of them! Sean had obviously made up his mind.

Elizabeth and Mack left to return to their home and Kathleen, Mrs. Manley and Sean headed back to the boarding house. Maeve was bunking in Beth's room at Alicia's.

Christmas that year had been celebrated with joy, but their parting hugs left a bitter-sweet feeling in everyone's heart.

Chapter
Thirty-Six

Before he left Alicia and Arthur's that night, Sean arranged to speak with them about more personal subjects in a few days. He was going to ask them to become legal guardians for Beth until she reached twenty-one. Also, he planned to give them the key to his safety deposit box at a bank downtown. He'd placed the original packet of information pertaining to his land and his Will there for safekeeping.

The boarding house felt warm and comforting as Kathleen, Mrs. Manley and Sean walked up the outdoor steps and into the front hall. Kathleen hugged them both, excused herself, said goodnight and left to go to bed. Mrs. Manley sat down with a sigh. "Sean, why don't you pour us each a brandy?"

He complied as she added a small log to the fire. They chatted comfortably about the baby, the delicious dinner and the good time everyone had enjoyed together. Then she turned to Sean, "Why on earth haven't you told me any of your plans? I couldn't believe my ears! California, of all places!" Tears trickled down her cheeks as she spoke.

He felt concerned and stunned as he looked at her, "Why, Wilma, I simply wanted to tell you all at the same time. Why are you so upset? I thought you'd be happy for me."

She drew a handkerchief from her sleeve and wiped her eyes and face, trying to get herself under control. "Sean, I thought we were becoming close and I saw the possibility of a future together."

Despite knowing it was too soon after her husband's death, Wilma had fallen in love with this kind and gentle man. She adored Kathleen and thought of her as another daughter.

Distressed, Sean took her hand in his. "Wilma, I am so sorry. You and I have become good friends. You've often mentioned how you miss your husband, and I've told you so much about Maggie and Frank. You've shared my worries about Dorothy and have been an amazing listener. I don't think I could have stayed anywhere else and felt so welcome. You've sheltered me during a worrisome and very traumatic time. I never meant to lead you on or give you the wrong impression." He shook his head sadly as he finished speaking.

She withdrew her hand from his and sat up straight. "I'm a selfish, lonely woman. We seemed so comfortable together. You haven't suggested anything more or been improper, Sean. My mind and heart skipped ahead of my common sense. It's simply been so comforting having a good man like you around the house. You've filled the loneliness I have felt since Joe died. Maybe we've healed each other. Let's call it a night and wait until morning to discuss this further. I shouldn't have brought it up tonight, but you shocked me with your plans to leave so soon. Goodnight. Sleep well."

Sean sat alone with his thoughts. Perhaps he should have seen this coming. He and Wilma were friends. That was all and his conscience was clear. He purposely hadn't hinted anything to her or his family about his future plans, thinking it best to get everything solidly in place first. He'd honestly believed it was best to tell them all together, so no one would feel excluded or left out.

Sean lay in bed that night, playing the wonderful events of Christmas Day over and over in his mind. He often chatted with Maggie before he fell asleep and, as the pale, winter moon cast a soft, white light across his bed, he whispered, "Maggie, girl, you'll be carried in my heart when I head for California. It will feel good to work with the land again. You always knew my dreams. Good night, my love."

Chapter
Thirty-Seven

A few days after Christmas, Sean and Maeve sat talking and catching up with each other. During the midst of their family gatherings, there hadn't been the opportunity for them to speak alone, so they'd planned to meet at Kathleen's favourite little tea room. Spending precious time together was always important, but the occasions were rare and far between. Maeve was returning to Montreal to continue her nursing career and her father was heading west. Chances were they might not meet again for a long time.

As father and daughter sat in the peaceful atmosphere of the sunny tea room, Maeve revealed some interesting information, news she'd been wanting to tell him for quite a while. A few months ago, she had written to the Red Cross, seeking any information available concerning the sad events surrounding Frank's death. Time passed, then one day a letter arrived from the young ambulance driver who'd moved Frank from the battlefield to the emergency hospital. He'd taken time to talk with several of the soldiers, the survivors who'd served under her brother. The story he told in that letter was very poignant and sad. He stressed the fact that Frank had fought and died alongside men who loved and respected him. She knew her brother was special, but somehow, hearing that others thought so too was a great comfort. Maeve felt that such a thoughtful letter should not go unanswered. His words touched her heart and she and Cliff began corresponding. Eventually, they had made plans to meet in Montreal after the war. As they sat enjoying afternoon tea together, Maeve handed Cliff's initial letter to her father.

Sean's eyes were moist as he read and re-read the letter, then handing it back to her, he said, "Thanks, Maeve. We all loved Frank. Nothing can bring him back to us, but it's comforting to learn that he shared his wisdom and talents with the other soldiers as he brought moments of joy and peace to them. Knowing this gives us a different sense of closure. War seems so senseless, but those young soldiers believed they were protecting their loved ones at home."

He paused, then said, "I'm suspecting that you and Cliff have met?"

Maeve answered, "Yes, Dad, his family lives in Montreal. The war ended and he contacted me soon after he returned. This is for you from Cliff."

With those words, she handed a small parcel to Sean. It held Frank's officer's sash, his identification tag, and two sketches he'd drawn. One was of an unknown soldier. The other was of Sean. Overcome with emotion, Sean reached across the table and held his daughter's hand. "Thank you. I will treasure these."

Leaving the tea room, they strolled toward the lakeshore. There was still so much catching up to do. Maeve shared her mixed emotions about Sean's plans to travel alone to California. She realized he had his own life to lead, but it seemed so far away.

"Dad, like everyone else, I was surprised by your news. I'm cautiously pleased for you and definitely understand why you've left Beth in Alicia and Arthur's care. At first, it seemed so final, asking them to become her guardians, but then I realized it wouldn't be fair to take her with you. She's happy at school and has already made friends. She'll be an excellent teacher someday. Alicia is obviously pleased to have her living in their home and I know they need authorization if they have to make decisions on her behalf. I'll write to her often and she's already agreed to visit me in Montreal. My friends are eager to meet this 'kid sister' of mine. They know how I feel about her."

Sean smiled as he replied. "You've eased my mind, Maeve. I worried that you might be the one who'd object to me leaving Beth in Toronto."

"Dad, life has dished out some very rough times for our family. We've also had special, wonderful times. As a nurse, I'm exposed to life and its problems every day. Health and happiness are two very powerful conditions. Without health, you can't enjoy very much. Without happiness, there's nothing. Health can be maintained to a certain degree by proper diet, exercise and mental attitude, yet there are an amazing number of people who simply do not understand this. Of course, humans are vulnerable to many insidious diseases and ailments that maim or snuff out life and we have no control over these. Happiness is different. It comes from deep within. I've witnessed examples of people who have everything to live for, they have no specific ailment, yet they are sick and unhappy. Perhaps I'm getting too set in my ways, but I do understand what is important in life. One must have pride in self. If you're unable to help yourself, you can't help anyone else. Oh dear, there I go, preaching again!"

Sean laughed. "Maeve, you've always been a wise, old soul! This is a marvellous time of your life. You are constantly learning new ideas and facts. As time goes on, you'll find yourself questioning the theories you're holding fast to right now. The important factor is to keep broadening yourself, without losing your personal goals, healthy outlook, or individual uniqueness. Each one of us is special. I can't tell you how many times I've had to stop, step back and re-establish my own self-worth!"

They walked along in silence, each lost in thought. It was an interlude, a special moment in time, one they'd both remember for a long time.

Chapter
Thirty-Eight

Sean and Wilma said goodbye with a hug, promising to keep in touch. He headed off to the little house on Webb Avenue, where a family farewell dinner was planned. He wanted his picture of their farewell to be of them seated around the table together, not waving from a crowded platform at the train station.

Sean departed on the lengthy train trip, from the Canadian shores of Lake Ontario to the shores of the Pacific in California.

Many of his fellow travellers were also heading west, seemingly driven by a common sense of adventure. He listened to their stories as the miles passed.

One man told of his plans to work at a vineyard, where his brother was the foreman. He told Sean that many of the pickers arrived seasonally to work at the various farms. They were called migrant workers, as most of them came from Mexico, seeking work wherever they could find it. Life was not easy for these employees or for those who hired them. There was the constant threat that a competitive farmer might offer a slightly higher wage and the pickers tended to move on when tempted. Then there was the ongoing hassle to market their product, be it onions, other vegetables or wine, as buyers attempted to push the prices down. Sean listened and learned, remembering problems that had occurred in Ireland.

The train travelled through forests, passing villages and cities, eventually reaching the flat prairies. Acres of farms and scrub lands revealed the vastness of the country as it unfurled before Sean's eyes. Days later, they reached the foothills of the awesome, rugged, and breathtakingly beautiful Rocky Mountain range. Frightening moments occurred as the train curved around and through the mountains, eventually safely arriving at the valleys beyond. In some areas, the rolling fields formed a patchwork quilt of colours. Sean's train ride ended in San Francisco, where he planned to take a bus for the remainder of the trip.

He sat in the station collecting his thoughts, studying the directions he'd been sent. According to this map, his property was located near San Francisco in a place called Napa Valley. He decided to purchase bus tickets and be on his way. It was early in the day and he was anxious to get on with his life.

As the bus left the city limits, they passed areas that grew both oak trees and evergreens. Ancient sequoias added to the overall beauty. Viewing the countryside, his mind eagerly anticipated the day's final destination. Late in the afternoon, the bus pulled up and stopped. The driver informed him that the farm marked on his map was located nearby. Sean picked up his luggage, thanked the driver and left the bus. It pulled away, leaving a trail of dust in its wake.

Brilliant shades of yellow and orange splashed across the western sky as the sun dipped toward the horizon. Sean turned and walked toward a small general store. An elderly man sat rocking on a large wooden porch.

"Good afternoon, sir. Is this Angel Town?"

The man continued rocking, eyeing Sean from head to toe. "Yup."

Sean took the map out of his pocket and handed it to the man. "Could you please tell me how far it is to this piece of land?"

"Yup, just go down that trail back of the store about two or three miles. You can't miss it. Leave your things here. I'll watch 'em for you." He paused, then added, "If I were you, I'd line up a bed for the night. That place across the street is my daughter's. She'll feed you a good meal and give you a place to sleep for a small price."

Realizing this was probably good advice, Sean turned to cross the street.

"Hey, wait a minute. How be you head out yonder. I'll take your bag and book you a room. Don't stay too long. You don't wanna get stuck out there in the dark." He struggled to get up from the rocker as he spoke.

Surprised by the strange hospitality, Sean waved and strode off at a brisk walk. Half an hour later, he crossed the small stone bridge marked on his map and started searching for a specific land marker.

The gently rolling land refused to reveal the well-kept farm and vineyards his eyes were seeking. The only sound he heard other than the beating of his heart was the burbling of a small creek flowing under the bridge. Here and there, he saw remnants of vines, empty stalks that twisted on wooden supports. Where were the workers? Where were the grapevines? There must be some mistake.

He reached down and took a handful of soil in his hand, smelled it and closed his eyes. There was a scent of grapes. Opening his eyes, he watched the soil trickle through his fingers and fall back to the ground. His breathing quieted as he listened to the sounds of nature. He smiled to himself and headed back to Angel Town. He should have known that the old man was probably senile and had sent him on a wild goose chase.

When Sean arrived back at the store, there was the old man, still rocking in his chair.

Sean lifted his hand in a quiet salute as he crossed the dusty street to the old house. He was ready to relax and rest. Something smelled delicious and his stomach groaned with anticipation and a sudden appetite.

A freshly painted, hand-carved sign hung over the door. 'The Best Hotel in Angel Town.' Glancing around, he smiled, thinking, *That's probably because this is the only hotel in Angel Town!* Raising his hand to use the door knocker, a voice stopped him. "Come right in, the door's open."

He opened the door and stepped inside.

The tall, slim woman before him stood smiling, with her hand extended. As they shook hands, he found himself looking straight into huge, blue eyes, the colour of morning glories. Her black hair was streaked with white and was pulled into a single braid that hung down her back. Dressed in cream coloured slacks and a simple, long sleeved blue cotton blouse, she was elegant.

"Welcome to Angel Town. My name is Angelina, but most people call me Angel. Why don't you take a minute and slip out back to the well for a quick wash up. Here's a towel for you to use and then I'll show you your room. I've already taken your bag up there."

He felt much better after his hands, arms and face were refreshed by the cool water from the well. Lifting the dipper off a nearby hook, he filled it with water, drank every drop, and then filled it again. He recalled his father telling him that water was 'Adam's ale'. He hung the towel on the clothesline and returned inside. Following his nose to the kitchen, he stood on the threshold observing the large room. It still seemed spacious even though it was filled with furnishings. A large table with eight chairs sat by the windows, a sink and counter and cooler took up a corner near the back door, and one entire wall held an open fireplace with two rockers on each side. Angel was stirring a big pot on the large wood-burning stove. She replaced the spoon on a plate and turned toward him, removing her apron as she spoke. "We're going to sit on the back porch when Daddy gets here, but I'll show your room to you first. You look better. That water feels good, doesn't it?"

His room was clean and comfortable with a double bed, chair, dresser and a few other amenities. She left him there, welcoming him to return downstairs when he was ready. He put on a clean shirt, combed his hair and soon they were seated outside the kitchen on a small covered porch. She handed him a cold beer and opened one for herself.

He reached his beer toward hers and tapped them together, saying, "Here's to your good health. Thank you for the warm welcome. It certainly feels good to be done travelling and be able to sit for a while. I'm grateful you can put me up for the night."

"Well, I can find a room for you even if you stay longer. Business isn't great right now."

Chapter
Thirty-Nine

The beer quenched his thirst and his hunger was appeased with the delicious dinner of chicken and dumplings with gravy, mashed potatoes and fresh peas.

They moved outside onto the back porch after dinner, where the conversation proved to be less satisfying. Angel's father started things off by asking Sean how much land he'd purchased.

Sean went upstairs and came down with his official papers. He handed them to Chuck, who glanced at them and shook his head. "How long ago did you say you purchased this land?"

"The date is right there on the final sale paper. Actually, it was just a month ago. Things moved very quickly. We corresponded by letter. Would you like me to show them to you?"

"Don't worry about it, son. I can see by the postmark that they were mailed around here. A lot of area folks pick up and mail their letters from my store. I hate to say it, but you've probably been dealing with a shyster. They're a dime a dozen. Sadly, there are lots of suckers too. You're one of many."

Angel spoke up, "A young fellow rides through here on horseback, carrying and picking up mail from different farms in the area. That land you think you've bought has been tied up in an estate ever since the government passed the Prohibition Act. A lot of the wineries in California were forced to close, including that big one near here. A few vintners are surviving by making grape juice. It's been quite a time. Some vineyards were uprooted and wine cellars were destroyed."

Sean shook his head. "I can hardly believe this. Everything seemed to be legal and in order. I'm at a loss what to do. Why are you two still here?"

Angel explained, "My husband is working in San Francisco. Mom died a few months ago, so Dad and I stayed here together. We still get a few customers at the store and I'm hoping to keep our home. Things are bound to change. It makes sense to rent the rooms out whenever someone turns up here. Our two sons have moved back East with their families."

Angel offered to go with Sean to look more carefully at the property the following day. He accepted her offer, thanked them both, wished them a goodnight and went upstairs to bed.

His goodnight words to Maggie were, "Well, I'm here, Maggie. Now what?" Sheer fatigue put him to sleep.

Chapter
Forty

Sean wakened to the aroma of bacon frying. Grabbing a towel, he hurried outside to the well. It didn't take long before he was shaved, dressed and seated in the kitchen. Chuck was already over at the store as he'd eaten his breakfast earlier.

Angel told him that her father rose with the sun each morning. After eating, he usually swept the porch at the store, lined up brooms, shovels and a few other articles that were for sale, against the outside wall. He'd followed this practice for years, wanting to be ready when the customers arrived. Nowadays, it was a long wait.

They chatted for a while longer as Sean ate breakfast, then Angel excused herself, saying, "I'm going to hang out the wash, then I'll go see that land with you."

Sean offered to help tidy up, but she suggested, "If you plan to stay a few days, you might just as well unpack and give your clothes an airing. I'll call upstairs and let you know when I'm ready."

He didn't have much to unpack, so he was ready when Angel called to say that it was time to go.

The air still held a hint of the night-time coolness as they waved to Chuck and turned down the trail. As they walked, Angel named several of the flowering shrubs, explaining the medical usage of some. One in particular, aloe, had a fluid inside that was used to heal many skin ailments, especially burns. She was knowledgeable and interesting.

When they reached the bleak-looking area he'd viewed the previous day, Sean turned to her, saying, "Now what?"

Angel motioned for him to follow her as she crossed over the pathway and entered the remains of the vineyard.

"Come over here. I want to show you something and tell you a story." She took a knife from her pocket, reached down and cut a piece of the vine away. "What do you see? Here, take hold of it and really look at it."

As he held the broken splice, he noted there was life in it. "So, it's not quite dead. How's that going to help me?"

Angel kept walking on toward a building he hadn't noticed last night. When they reached it, she pushed the large wooden door open and they both stepped inside. A large wine press stood before them. Empty kegs were neatly stacked against a back wall. She led him to another doorway and opened it. A stairway led down into a surprisingly cool, damp-smelling area. There were many shelves in front of them. Some still held full bottles of wine.

Without speaking, she headed back up the stairs and motioned for him to come and sit beside her on a bench. "Sean, I've just shown you the remnants of what used to be a very successful business. The building and most of the equipment are in good repair. Everyone picked up and left when the inability to sell their product finished them. They were broke and disheartened. Since then, a few years have passed. Recently we've heard rumours that the owners returned to the East, and two of them have since died."

She stopped speaking, letting her words sink in. Then she continued. "I'm a pretty good judge of people. So's my Dad. We talked this over last night and have a proposition for you. These people purchased a large number of acres from us, but they haven't paid us yet. Practically speaking, we could put up a pretty good fight to gain our land back along with everything on it. How would you like to join forces? These vines need work. A lot of work. We need a man who's good with people. Rumour has it that Prohibition will soon end. We'd like to start preparing as soon as possible. Will you come on board and give us a hand?"

Sean couldn't believe his ears. He simply sat and stared at her for a few moments as his emotions got the better of him.

Angel smiled, saying, "Look, I know I'm throwing a lot at you all at once. Believe me, this isn't a spur of the moment plan for us. We've been putting our thoughts together for quite a while. I was planning to return to 'Frisco with my husband after his next visit home, specifically to search for a suitable man to work with us. We'd like to offer you the opportunity of managing the business with us. Eventually, if all goes well, it could lead to a part ownership too. What are your thoughts?"

Sean shook her hand. "I'm in if you want me. At this point, what have I got to lose? You really are an Angel!"

Chapter
Forty-One

Two days later, Sean and Angel headed for San Francisco to meet with her husband, Willy. The tall, silver-haired man welcomed them to his office with a firm handshake. Angel hadn't mentioned that Willy was an architect and a contractor. Two photos of completed projects decorated one wall of his office.

"Welcome, Sean. Angel tells me you are quite possibly the man we need to oversee the next step of our exciting project. I believe in getting right down to business. We'll go over everything with you today. It's my understanding, based on some very dependable sources, that Prohibition will end within the next five years. In the meantime, we have work to do. Everything is 'in place' on paper. Come and take a look at the overview of our future winery business."

An amazing design was spread on a table by the window. Slightly overwhelmed, Sean realized that this was no dream. Here before him was the reality. Willy pointed at his vision of the completed project as he described the plans.

"The new vineyards will be planted here, where there's enough acreage to expand. This building will house a new wine press and a wine cellar, with extra space for the wine to be aged and stored. The kegs will be kept over here. These two buildings are bunkhouses for the workers. This facility will be the reception area where tours, wine tastings, a gift shop and restaurant will be placed. Any questions so far?"

"When do you plan to start working on this amazing project?" Sean asked.

Angel answered, "Immediately. Willy and I have our plan of action on the board over here. We've already purchased a couple of house trailers for the initial employees to live in until their proper housing is completed. In the meantime, the planting will begin as soon as the area is prepared. The people we hire will either work the land for planting, or construct the buildings, depending on their expertise. The grapes are the foundation of this business, so naturally, they are our priority. Come and look at the completed winery in miniature."

She walked over to a sturdy table which held the tiny replicas of the access road, acres of grapevines and the buildings. Everything was built to an exact scale. Sean gazed at the model of the perfect winery and realized he was getting a glimpse into the future. His heart pounded with excitement.

Willy directed him to check out a list that was posted on a bulletin board on the wall:

1) Hire a manager

2) Hire the initial work crew

3) Complete bunkhouses

4) Order the new wine press

5) Construct the main work building (wine cellar, keg storage, press room)

6) Order grapevines

Planting guidelines:

1. Select a site with full or part sun.

2. Prepare soil; deep, well-drained and loose.

3. Good air circulation is a necessity.

4. Space vines 6 to 10 feet apart (16 feet for muscadines).

5. For each vine, dig a planting hole 12 inches deep and 12 inches wide.

6. Fill with 4 inches of topsoil.

7. Trim off broken roots.

8. Set the vine into the hole, slightly deeper than it grew in the nursery.

9. Cover the roots with 6 inches of soil and tamp down.

10. Fill with the remaining soil, but don't tamp this down.

11. Prune the top back to two or three buds at planting time.

As Sean stood reading the lists, Willy laughed, saying, "Most workers in this area know how to plant grapevines. These points were meant for our new manager. We didn't know who we'd end up hiring, so Angel and I figured this was useful information for any overseer to know."

Angel opened the basket lunch she'd brought for them. As they sat, enjoying their food and the lovely view overlooking San Francisco Bay, Angel turned toward Sean, saying, "Willy had our lawyer write up a contract for our manager a few weeks ago. As I mentioned to you, we planned to interview several people this week. We'd like to give you the contract now. I know you have tentatively said yes, but everything has been verbal. Take time to read it this afternoon, then you'll probably know if you want the job or not. If you do, it's yours. Meanwhile, we'll make plans to have the papers signed tomorrow, with our lawyer present, at Willy's office. You can give us your final decision at dinner tonight. Does that suit you, Sean?"

Sean nodded his head in agreement.

Sean went over the document carefully a couple of times. Then he set it down, allowing the words sink in. He already knew what his answer would be.

That evening, at dinner, Sean's voice was husky as he said, "Thank you for giving me this wonderful opportunity."

The papers were signed at Willy's office the following morning and reservations were made for a special, celebratory dinner.

That evening, they were welcomed by the maître d' who led the trio up a flight of stairs to a small, elegant, private dining room, overlooking the city lights. A bottle of champagne was brought to their table, the cork was popped, the glasses filled, and then Angel and Willy stood up. They toasted Sean, their guest of honour, welcoming him as the new manager of the Angel Town Winery.

Later, Sean prepared for bed, then walked to the window in his room. A full moon shone on the waters of the bay, forming a path that seemed to lead straight to him. As he stood admiring the magic of the moon, he thought of his family. Throughout the years, after their bedtime stories, he and Maggie would tuck them in, listen to their prayers and say goodnight.

Whenever the moon lit up the darkened room, he'd say to them, "Wherever you are, in your own little corner of the world, look at the moon, ponder the beauty and think of each other. Always remember that the same moon shines on each one of us."

With those thoughts, he whispered, "Goodnight, sweet Maggie. I'm going to find Dorothy. Life is full of dreams that are coming true. I sense you know that. And Maggie, tonight the moon is full."

Chapter
Forty-Two

During Sean's first year, a designated section of land was tilled and prepared for the initial planting of the grapevines. His days passed quickly as the hours were filled with hard work and a wonderful sense of accomplishment.

Recognizing that it was wise to seek an income from the land as soon as possible, Sean made a few suggestions during one of the get-togethers that he, Angel, Chuck and Willy held regularly. They scheduled this time to visit and discuss business, but the atmosphere was always informal as they sat on the porch at the bed and breakfast. Sean made his proposal by showing them a rough design of vegetable and fruit crops. He clarified that some would produce an income quickly, while others would take a longer time to grow. He also presented a cost effective budget for the funds needed to do the preparation of the land and the initial planting. He had done his homework well. They were excited and very impressed, so they gave Sean the go-ahead to prepare the land and purchase the necessary plants and seeds. He asked Willy to have a more formal plan drawn up. Meanwhile, he would proceed with the physical preparations.

Within weeks, a large vegetable garden was planted on one section of the land. Brussel sprouts, broccoli, carrots, eggplants, garlic, melons, squash and tomatoes were chosen as the first vegetables to plant. Each row was well-spaced, allowing room for growth as well as access for weeding and picking. Eventually, the vegetable garden area was surrounded by strawberry plants and several rows of raspberry bushes. Finally, an orchard of young apple trees was planted in groupings of six around the outer perimeter. A few lemon trees were also introduced to the area.

The vegetable garden produced its gifts very quickly. These foods were used for their households, the bed and breakfast and the workers. The surplus products were sold at a covered stand that was built near Chuck's store. This attractive farm fresh market fit perfectly into their plans for the town. Fortunately, the river that ran through the property provided an ongoing supply of water. It adequately fulfilled the needs of the entire growing area, including both the gardens and the vineyards.

Angel Town gradually changed from a sleepy dot on the map to a bustling town. The area outside of San Francisco was expanding. Automobiles provided easy access to the outlying districts. Along with their dreams and plans to claim the vineyard properties back, they also wanted to improve the properties that they lived on. Angel's bed and breakfast was in demand. In fact, she often had to turn prospective guests away. These changes had been anticipated; consequently, their original plans for the vineyards and the winery had included projects to update the existing buildings and to design new ones.

The quaint atmosphere they wished to create and maintain for Angel Town was strictly enforced. The surrounding area was surveyed and divided into a defined business area, park, and generous housing lots. The roadways were wide and lined with palm trees. When the lots were sold, each sale was completed only when the purchasers presented building plans that were in accordance with the town's architectural specifications. No plans, no purchase. These restrictions drew a certain type of buyer to the area. Talented artisans arrived, anxious to live in these picturesque, wide open spaces that appealed to their creative natures. Retirees seeking warmth travelled from the Northern States and Canada. Young families arrived, hoping to find a less expensive home away from the city.

During the same time, there was ongoing activity in the outskirts of town as the winery buildings were gradually constructed. Sean felt a new sense of belonging when his own house was completed. His home was within a comfortable walking distance from the main winery building, providing both privacy as well as a comfortable proximity to the business. He planted bougainvillea vines, a lemon tree and an herb garden within his first week of occupancy.

Four years after the initial planting, the first harvesting of the grapes was celebrated. Angel, Chuck, Sean, Willy, the full time-workers, and their families formed a small excited group. They stood watching as the new press crushed the first baskets of fruit. A cheer went up and a few eyes misted when everything went smoothly. Several baskets of grapes were placed in a large container outside. Six of the Mexican workers removed their shoes, rolled up their pants, stepped into the mass of fruit and performed a rowdy but victorious 'dance of the grapes!'

A wonderful buffet of food was set up inside the main building. The tables were decorated with beautiful whole vegetables and milk bottles that held sprays of wisteria. A few bottles of well-aged wine from the old winery had been brought up from the cellars, dusted and placed on a special table. They sat waiting to be opened and poured into glasses to celebrate their success. It was a joyful occasion.

During the following days, some of the grape juice was bottled, labelled and prepared for immediate sale under the name 'Angelic Grape Juice.' A portion of the initial squeezed product was placed in oak barrels to ferment.

The company began making and bottling varieties of specialty wines, neatly storing them in the expansive new wine cellars. They had time to taste, test and perfect their product. Not an ounce of wine was sold as the company strictly followed the law; however, they planned to be ready whenever the Prohibition ban was eventually over.

The landscape continued to change as the vineyards were slowly expanded. Row upon row of healthy vines flourished under the California skies.

Meanwhile, their vegetable and fruit sales increased. Some of the new home and business owners eagerly worked in the gardens, anxious to earn extra funds to help them sustain their own ventures. When the orchard produced its first crop of apples, students from the city were bussed to the area to work in the gardens. They were also eager to earn money weeding, picking vegetables or berries by day and returning to 'Frisco at night. As the vineyards expanded, more migrant workers were hired.

Chapter
Forty-Three

Angel Town Winery was planning to be well-prepared when the Prohibition Act was repealed. The vineyard was thriving. The wine cellars were stocked, shelves filled with wine bottles containing the individual varieties of wines, both red and white. They were labelled and ready for sale. When the gates were finally opened to visitors, the tours and tastings began. The staff was well-trained and knowledgeable.

Business grew rapidly. Buses of tourists arrived, eager to spend a few hours learning about the history of wine-making. They were interested in the process of growing and harvesting the grapes, as well as the overall wine-making process. Wine tastings were offered and then a delicious lunch was served in the outdoor restaurant. Bougainvillea and wisteria climbed trellises, lending their beauty and scent to the dining area.

One sunny day, Sean stood watching a busload of tourists arrive. The driver stopped the bus in front of the reception centre, allowing his passengers to disembark before continuing on to the designated parking area. The people were guided into the building by one of their employees. Smiling, he turned and began walking toward his house, located a leisurely ten minute walk from the busy area. He still felt a sense of wonder as he followed the road that led him past a lower section of the vineyard. His eyes lifted to the gentle hills where row upon row of grapevines grew.

When he originally accepted the position as the manager, he understood that he was facing a mammoth job. The original choice of the grape varieties eventually became his responsibility, but initially, selections were decided upon by Angel, Chuck and Willy. They knew which varieties were best for the climate and location. In time, his practical education, as well as the formal studying he pursued, enhanced his knowledge. He quickly learned the importance of choosing the right plants, then overseeing the planting in the fertile, well-drained soil. Today, as an experienced vintner, he understood everything about the wine-making business.

Chapter
Forty-Four

Sean and Alicia's correspondence was sporadic, but at least they were in touch. She wrote that Kathleen and Beth had pursued their educations. Kathleen was now working in business and Beth was teaching. They were both married and lived in Fort Erie. Maeve still lived in Montreal, working as a nurse, and was also married. He learned that he had grandchildren.

In his letters, Sean explained to Alicia that his few attempts to locate Dorothy been unsuccessful. He had followed one clue all the way to Los Angeles, but nothing came of it. Every question regarding her whereabouts proved to be fruitless.

Elizabeth and Mack continued writing to him every few months. The interesting letters told him of their wonderful trips to England, Ireland and Scotland. Each letter brought a touch of home and the past to him. He considered travelling back to Canada, but as the years passed, his responsibilities kept him rooted in Angel Town.

One day, the post brought a sad letter from Elizabeth, telling Sean that Dr. Mack had died during the past summer. A sudden, massive heart attack had struck him down while they were vacationing at their cottage north of Toronto. Elizabeth's note was brief. She apologized for not letting him know sooner, but he sensed her grief at the loss of this wonderful man.

Saddened and shocked to hear this news, Sean sat down and answered her letter, expressing his sympathy. They continued their correspondence. She filled her letters with stories about his children and their ever-growing family. He wrote telling her about the wonderful work that was being accomplished in Angel Town.

When Elizabeth mentioned in one letter that she had decided to come to California for a visit, he'd responded eagerly. Now, he was scheduled to pick her up at the airport in San Francisco later that day.

Thinking about this, deep in concentration, he continued down the road toward his house. Suddenly he glanced up, noticing that two women were walking toward him. Something about them seemed vaguely familiar. They both waved, then the taller one ran toward him. He watched in amazement. No! It couldn't be!

Dorothy threw herself into his arms, crying, "Dad, it is you! I wrote home a year or so ago. Alicia answered my letter. I've been corresponding with her ever since. Elizabeth has also been writing to me, and told me of her planned trip to California. She arrived a few days ago and has been staying in a hotel within walking distance of where I live. She rented a car and drove me here today."

Tears flowed as Dorothy and Sean hugged. It had been a long time since they'd seen each other, but as he held his daughter, it seemed like yesterday.

He turned toward the beautiful, white-haired woman who stood a few steps back, tactfully giving father and daughter a few special moments together.

He spoke as his eyes met hers, "How can I ever thank you, Elizabeth?"

She simply smiled and shook her head. "It's been a miracle for all of us, Sean. Hearing from Dorothy after so many years has added a wonderful, new dimension to our lives. Mack was so pleased when we heard from her. "

Elizabeth was here and she'd found Dorothy. As they turned and walked toward the house, Sean's heart was full of gratitude and love.

CPSIA information can be obtained
at www.ICGtesting.com
Printed in the USA
FFOW02n1718070216
21131FF

9 781460 262566